The Miracle
of the
HERMIT CRAB

The Miracle
of the
HERMIT CRAB

The miracle given by Jesus to a young boy stricken with cerebral palsy

Dwight G. Alexander

The Miracle of the Hermit Crab

Published by
Inscript Publishing
a division of Dove Christian Publishers
P.O. Box 611
Bladensburg, MD 20710-0611
www.inscriptpublishing.com

Copyright © 2018 by Dwight G. Alexander

Cover Design by Mark Yearnings

Cover Photographs by Dwight Alexander

All rights reserved. No part of this publication may be used or reproduced without permission of the publisher, except for brief quotes for scholarly use, reviews or articles.

Except where noted, Scripture quotes are from the Holy Bible, New International Version®, NIV® Copyright ©1973, 1978, 1984, 2011 by Biblica, Inc.® Used by permission. All rights reserved worldwide.

ISBN: 9781732112544

Printed in the United States of America

Dedication

This book is dedicated to our daughters Margarette 'Maggie' Alexander, Talitha 'Balz' Alexander, Ja-el 'OB' Alexander, and Janel 'Dilbi' Alexander. Your only brother developed Cerebral Palsy at an early age. Unfortunately, you never enjoyed his full companionship as a healthy brother who can play ball with you, run your errands, climb trees for you, or do other things normal kids do. I had hoped he would be someone you can play with, celebrate with, and eventually, be a man who would help you in many ways as a brother. All our plans and hopes seemed to have gone south; however, God is mighty and supreme in all his ways. We have been tremendously blessed by Anzic's presence in our lives, and I know you have also when you are around him. He still provides love, friendship, laughter, joy, and most importantly, his adoration for each of you. I know you love him dearly and care for him like no other. He will always be a part of your life and will always provide the moral support we all need.

In writing this book, I hope I conveyed the way the Lord was molding our lives using Anzic. His grace, his love, his mercy, his forgiveness, his corrections, his discipline, and his relationship as a father to us was revealed in the most visible way through Anzic's life, and we have been tremendously blessed. By embracing Anzic and spending time with him, you will also experience God in an amazing way and he will reveal to you how much he cares and loves each of you. Anzic's disability is a constant reminder of how much we need each other and how much more we need God.

We were all especially selected and set aside by God to be taught greater lessons through Anzic, and for that, we will always be grateful for his life.

We love you always,
Mom and Dad
Clarinda & Dwight G. Alexander

Foreword

When asked by the author, Dwight Alexander, who is a Christian brother and coworker in God's ministry, a family friend, and a relative, to write a foreword to this book, "The Miracle of the Hermit Crab" I elatedly agreed to contribute my twosenses on his writing. Little did I know that I would struggle to fulfill my commitment to the author because of how powerfully inspiring this book is and how it emotionally provoked me to frequent tears by the enduring challenges in Anzic's life and how it served as a beacon of contentment, hope and joy for others to feed on. I have known Dwight Alexander for several years, along with his wife Clarinda, who is closely related to me through a different genealogical path, and their family. The author's writing reflects his persona of moral character, love, humility, and honesty that are fundamental assets to desired growth in familial relationships. I am humbly blessed to have known the main subject in his story, his beloved son Anzic Alexander, whose life experiences and events have taken me in awe of his capacity to inspire his father, family, and others to appreciate the amazing works of God displayed over and over again through him. His life and journey through series of medical consultations and treatments in Palau and Hawaii involved critical participations by his father, mother, siblings, family helper, medical care givers, and others. And his interactions and relationships with those involved have drawn our attention to also appreciate the value of family and loving sacrifices we must offer to sprout and sustain family bonding.

The author chronicles a beautiful story of his son, who is with physical disabilities and limitations, yet his limitations do not constrain his flourishing personality, character and spirit. I truly believe that Anzic is a beautifully created and unique child of God, and special in the eyes of God and lives he has impacted.

No love is greater than that of a father for his son. This

book transports readers like you and me to Palau where a father, along with his wife and three daughters, invites us on a downtoearth, narrative story of his gifted son, whose plight is about seeking health restoration. It can move the readers to tears as it tells of detailed, bucketful of Anzic's distressing medical ailment and delicate therapies that brought on discomfort, agony, doubt, emotional and spiritual burden upon the family. And by the same token, Anzic's quest for solution to his ailment brought about spiritual growth and strength, contentment in what comes our way, healing and display of miracles by which God's grace and love is expressed through his struggles and personality. Throughout the book, his medical journey fed on an intimate, loving relationships especially with his father, mother, and siblings. It inspires us to enhance our understanding of our relationship with our loving God who understands our own limitations, difficulties and challenges in life, and to entrust our life's struggles and uncertainties to His love and care. After all, don't we all have disabilities and limitations in one sense or another? Thus, we can be truly blessed by patiently waiting on God's power and deliverance, as He is always in control over all things concerning our lives. As the story unfolds, one can see and reap the practical lessons on a selfless devotion and love which the father displays throughout the book.

Furthermore, this book is particularly a heartbreaking story of special, loving relationship between Anzic and his father, as lived and caught through the lens of the father's eyes. And so no one else could have been able to write Anzic's story but his own father. It tells of the difficult times when the parents seemed helpless in situations like seeing their son in pain and in need of care and comfort, in upsetting and worrying occasions that call for self examination of our faith and trust in God concerning things beyond our control, as well as shining moments that Anzic blesses the hearts of people around him through his ability to sing songs of praise or simply express his thrills and excitements. Furthermore, Anzic's physical limitations and joyful heart has affected his family and others in enabling them to witness God's amazing works in and through his life.

I definitely recommend this book to everyone. Adults, families, and special education teachers will find this book a gold mine of personal experiences and lessons to understand, accept, and participate in the life of a child or family member with limitations and disabilities, for moral courage, sensitivity, empathy, and creativity. This book will constantly remind us of our dire need of God's daily intervention in all circumstances of our lives. The good news is, God has always been with Anzic in all his situations and in control of everything. As with the story of a man born blind in the Gospel of John, Chapter 9, God has indeed displayed His amazing works in Anzic! I hope, through Anzic's story, that you too may be drawn nearer to God in your struggles!

Uchel R. Naito

Table of Contents

Dedication ... v

Foreword ... vi

Shriners Children's Hospital ... 1

Anzic's Operation Throws a Curve Ball ... 15

God Gives Anzic a Better Treatment ... 27

The Surgery Is Postponed Yet Again ... 34

Anzic's Early Years ... 43

The Year after the First Hip Surgery ... 52

Anzic's Sister Dilbi ... 58

Anzic's Favorite Activities ... 64

Back to the Drawing Board ... 76

The Second Miracle ... 87

God's Purpose and Will ... 96

About This Book's Title ... 106

1

Shriners Children's Hospital

As I stood in the hallway with my wife and Mr. Uchel Naito (a worker in the Palau Referral Coordinating Office in Honolulu, as well as a deacon in his church), we watched my son Anzic being pushed on his bed toward the operating room of the Shriners Children's Hospital in Honolulu. I had a tremendous feeling of helplessness. As much as my wife and I love Anzic, there's a line where we stop, and Anzic goes forward into the hands and care of others. The realization that I could be helpless at critical moments of my children's lives was unnerving, to say the least. As parents, we want to be in control, and we want very much to know for certain the outcome of activities and events surrounding our children.

Mr. Naito, understanding our dilemma, spoke quietly: "Let us go to the cafeteria and eat while we wait." It was obvious there was nothing we could do but wait, as Anzic was in the hands of the doctors. This was a moment when all we could do was to trust the Lord that Anzic was in better hands than our own. As we walked down the hall toward the elevator, I quietly asked God to take care of Anzic for us and to help the doctors do a good job so that he would be able to enjoy life without constant pain.

We spoke little on that short journey to the hospital's cafeteria, as all three of us searched for words and stories to comfort each other as well as convince each other that Anzic would be all right. I figured we were going to need stories and perhaps a few devotional thoughts to pass the time while we awaited the outcome of the surgery.

I was reminded of the song taken from Psalm 46:10, "Be

still and know that I am God." Looking up this verse, I ran across the first verse of that psalm, which says, "God is our refuge and our strength, an ever-present help in time of trouble." And later it says, "The LORD Almighty is with us. The God of Jacob is our fortress" (46:7). I was calmed by reading the entire chapter. Meanwhile, Deacon Naito affirmed God's continual presence in our lowest moments. I looked to him as a leading authority in this area.

Several years before, Mr. Naito was a known authority in Palau—my homeland—with his education and achievements. He led the work in planning for Palau's water use and wastewater management—a critical work in small island states, ensuring that wastewater is managed properly to avoid sanitary issues. Back then, he was simply a church attendee, one of those guys who would sit in the pew throughout the service and leave just before the service ends. We wouldn't see him until the next Sunday, as he was engrossed in his work and community projects. Life changed for him and his wife, Ms. Allyn Takada, when he collapsed during a basketball game.

The constraints of the local hospital in Palau prevented the doctors from discovering Mr. Naito's ailment, and he was referred to Tripler Army Medical Center in Honolulu. When his illness was diagnosed and made known, he had to change many of his plans. The cost of medicine for his illness was too expensive for the Belau National Hospital as well as the local clinics and pharmacies in Palau to carry, and they were not able to support a steady supply of his medicine. Mr. Naito had to stay in Honolulu to ensure that the medicine he needed was available. He relocated to Hawaii with his wife and son.

Since then, Mr. Naito has almost fully recovered from this disease. We can say that this is a miracle and an act of grace from God. He has transitioned from a productive community life to a fruitful and meaningful church life, in which he serves as a deacon and performs pastoral work for a Palauan congregation called the Ungil Chais Fellowship (*ungil chais* means "good news"), under the Good Shepherd Church in Honolulu. He most certainly is a leading authority in understanding God's grace and mercy. Thus, his words of comfort and advice were comforting and brought understanding that God was indeed in control.

His wife, Allyn, serves as the medical coordinator for the Palau Referral Office in Honolulu. Many of the Palau patients traveling to Hawaii (as arranged through the medical coordinator's office) have terminal illnesses. The Lord has used Mr. Naito to shed His light and to comfort patients with His holy Word.

So, it was a great comfort just having Mr. Naito near us at this time. When he spoke, I could almost sense that the Lord was speaking to us through him. It was reassuring and comforting.

I thought back to the day Anzic was born, when the nurse who delivered him shouted with joy, "It's a boy!" That was April 8, 2007, and my wife had carried him to full term. I remembered thinking, "Certainly, things will be fine with this one." Anzic's older sister wasn't so fortunate, having been born six months into my wife's pregnancy. Right from the start, there had been problems due to her premature birth, and we are still dealing with some of the limitations and challenges in her growth and development.

However, Anzic was just as healthy as a baby can be. His eyes were bright and responsive to movements. His head would turn in response to sounds, showing that he heard and had a good sense of direction as to the origin of the sounds. His limbs and movements all indicated a healthy and strong baby.

My first gut reaction to the nurse's shouts of joy was ecstatic. Here was a child I could call *son*. A child I could take fishing and farming and do all the manly things with. Someone who would carry on my name and not have it changed when he gets married, and who would have children to carry on the family name even further.

My head was jumping far ahead of me. Would my son be a good basketball player? Would he like baseball? Volleyball? Would he like sports at all? Many things came through my head as to what my son would be like.

As the days went by, Anzic continued to have clear eyes, his hearing was sharp, and his responses and movements were all normal. My wife and I couldn't be happier. Finally, a son has been given to us, and he would carry on our name. We were so proud.

We closely watched him every day and had great joy in taking care of him. We didn't ignore our other children, but certainly, Anzic was the center of attention for everyone, including the older sisters. We gave him toys. We looked forward to his first words and his first step. We debated which word he would say first—*Mom* or *Dad*.

His mother was already planning where he would go to preschool and kindergarten. She was already envisioning him in Sunday school and church programs. She was already talking about him going on field trips. There were so many plans for him, even before he could eat or walk by himself.

As the months went by, we continued to observe each new development closely. We were assured in every hospital appointment that he would be a strong and healthy boy. Everything looked good, and we were anxious for him to grow up.

As we watched him grow, there were times when I had concerns I couldn't shake. I would look at him closely to see if there was something wrong with him. For example, I noticed that his mouth was always open, and he continued to drool. All my other children never had this problem. He appeared to be a little slow in his motions, with somewhat lazy movements. At times he seemed slow to respond and looked somewhat confused. While we prepared food, didn't bother us but chose to be by himself. This surprised us, because when our other children were this young, we had to constantly tell them to stay out of the kitchen; they were intrigued by food and wanted to get involved in the cooking, which caused big messes and made food preparation very difficult. But Anzic preferred just to be alone and watch TV.

I thought certainly that his appearance of weakness or laziness would raise red flags with the medical providers, but no caution came, and no alarm was raised. The continued assurances from the doctors erased my fears, and I looked past those challenges and what appeared to be abnormal behavior. I kept telling myself, "He's still young, and when he gets older, he'll be just like me."

The first real alarm came when Anzic was six months old. In Palau, when a child reaches the time to receive more than milk—to eat baby food and other soft foods—we bring the best food on the island for them. Often, it's the wild pigeon, a pricey delicacy that only rich and high-ranking community leaders enjoy during festivities. Although hunting pigeons is strictly prohibited by law, there are ways we can get them for the children when they have their first meal. The meat is a little tough, so they cannot chew it, since most children have few teeth at that time. But just sucking the juice out of the meat is fine. It's a source of pride that one's child, for their first meal, would eat the most sought-after food on the island, even though it's not the most pleasant sight, and maybe not very appetizing for a small child. The bird's feathers are plucked, and the bird is cleaned, but the head remains. Wild pigeons have this black round thing right above their beak which makes them look odd and different.

All my daughters had enjoyed wild pigeon for their first meal, so when it came time for Anzic's first meal, a wild pigeon was prepared for him. When we presented him his meal and the small pot was opened for him, he looked at the bird and showed disgust. He wanted nothing to do with it. He almost ran away from it.

This, as well as other events of that first year, were special times that we cherished, but they also raised questions about his condition and health.

By his second birthday, he still wasn't able to speak, eat solid food, or walk. We felt that maybe he needed medical intervention, but every time we brought this to the attention of the doctors, they would tell us that Anzic was growing normally and would eventually speak and walk. They said some children are quick to develop these skills while others are slower. "He's just one of the slow ones," they would say.

But to us as his parents, the fact that Anzic was two years old already and still unable to walk or speak was an alarming sign that he might not be as normal a child as we had hoped. Both my wife and I did some soul-searching as we tried to figure out what had happened. Many questions came rushing through our minds, which we sometimes discussed with friends and family. We asked questions: What brought this on Anzic? Was there any action on our part that might have caused it? Did we commit a serious sin that God was punishing us for? And most importantly, what exactly was wrong with our son?

From one doctor to another, we were given the same answer: Anzic was normal, and everything would be fine once he started to get these things in sync. So, we continued to hope, we continued to pray, and we continued to observe and watch.

In 2010, a team of doctors from the Shriners Children's Hospital in Honolulu came to Palau to treat children with bone problems. The Belau National Hospital, the government-run hospital in Palau and Anzic's hospital, called and informed us that they had made an appointment for Anzic with this team of visiting doctors.

The doctors examined Anzic and asked for x-rays and ultrasound tests and blood tests to be done. After these were completed and analyzed, we were called in to discuss the results. The doctors—politely and in the friendliest way possible—explained to us that Anzic's hip joints were growing outward and not inward. This meant that the ball of the thighbone (femur) was not in the hip socket where it was supposed to be, but rather outside it, and growing further out. As a result, it was painful for Anzic to cross his legs and even harder for him to walk. Each time he stood, his thigh bones were pushing against flesh near the hip area, causing great discomfort.

The doctors recommended that we try having Anzic sit cross-legged to try and push the thigh bone into the hip socket. But Anzic did not like sitting cross-legged. He often sat in the "W" position, where he bent his legs at the knees and sat on top of his legs, with his feet extending to each side. The doctors said this would push the bones out even more, and he needed to sit cross-legged.

Since Anzic always sat in the "W" position and had grown used to it, and was uncomfortable sitting cross-legged, we had a huge challenge on our hands—especially since we also realized that at times we weren't really communicating with him. It appeared that either he didn't really understand us, or he simply chose not to listen to us.

But the good news was that we finally knew why our son wasn't able to use his legs and why he wasn't able to walk. Our greater hope was that once the thigh bone ball went into the hip socket, he would be able to walk. Or would he?

I sensed that there were other medical problems surrounding Anzic's case—that even if the hip bones were fixed, he still might not be able to walk. There were so many uncertainties surrounding Anzic's condition that nothing was guaranteed at this point. There were other problems which we felt were not clearly explained to us—like his slowness to learn to speak and to respond properly to what we said. Our biggest concern was why he didn't like to eat solid foods, except for junk food. I even started to blame myself for giving him that wild pigeon that first time we tried to get him to eat.

I realized that Anzic must have an even more serious medical problem, but I didn't know what it was. Was this a curable illness? Was it a birth defect, and incurable? Was it a punishment from God? Could I or my wife be to blame?

During this time, I thought about the baby son of King David and Bathsheba, whom God decided to inflict with a disease because of David's sin with Bathsheba (2 Samuel 11-12). I sort of felt like David, and I sensed that I was getting a glimpse of David's agony over his son's illness. I placed myself in the same situation as David. Was it my sin that brought this on Anzic? If so, what kind of sin did I commit? I'd committed many terrible sins in my life—was it all of those, or a particular one? Did God not forgive me when I asked for forgiveness and turned my life to serve him?

I was confused. I wanted desperately to fall on my knees and scream so that God would reveal which sin was the real problem that brought this terrible condition on poor Anzic. I cried and begged God to heal Anzic.

I looked further at the events of David's story for clues, and to see if there was a way to appeal to God's mercy and grace to cure my son.

David and Bathsheba's son had become very sick and was about to die. David put on sackcloth and mourned over his son. The entire palace, seeing their king's agony, mourned with him. Everyone pleaded and begged God to grant their king his prayer for his son's healing. But God allowed this child to die (2 Samuel 12:13-23).

From the story, we can sense that Bathsheba was a beautiful woman who could immediately capture one's heart. She did exactly that with King David. Once Bathsheba informed David that she was pregnant, David began thinking of ways to cover their sin. He decided to have Bathsheba's husband, Uriah the Hittite, sent home from the frontlines. David hoped that when Uriah spent time with his wife, everyone would think Uriah fathered the child his wife carried. David must have hoped that even Uriah would think this, and it would hide the king's adulterous act with Bathsheba.

However, Uriah stayed outside the door of the king's house and slept there, refusing to go home to his wife; he felt guilty about going to lie with her while his men were still out fighting and enduring deprivations. Uriah was a man of honor and integrity, a man most worthy of respect, and one of King David's thirty most trusted valiant men.

Uriah's honorable behavior ruined David's plan. Now David's sin with Bathsheba would be revealed. They had committed adultery, which in Israel was punishable by death for both persons involved. It would not be good if the king of Israel were found to be guilty of adultery.

When the time came for Uriah's return to the battleground, David decided he must come up with a plan to get rid of Uriah. David wrote out his plan in a message to Joab, his battle strategist and general. He sent the message by Uriah.

David instructed Joab to put Uriah on the front edge of battle; then, once the battle heated up, Joab was to withdraw his men, leaving Uriah without backup so that he would get killed. This plan worked.

As soon as David received word that Uriah was dead, he sent for Bathsheba to move into his palace and become his wife. This looked like a gracious thing to do for a friend, but God knew the real motive. This was a sin in the eyes of God, and He was displeased with David.

God immediately sent the prophet Nathan to confront David about his sin. Nathan told David the story of a wealthy man with many sheep and a poor man with one ewe lamb. When the rich man had guests to feed, he decided to take the one ewe lamb from the poor man while sparing his own sheep. David realized the great injustice in the story. Not knowing that the story was directed at him, he angrily proclaimed that the rich man should be punished. David was stunned when Nathan told him that the evil man was none other than David himself. Nathan told the king how displeased God was with him for murdering Uriah and taking Bathsheba his wife. He said that as a result of this sin, David's newborn child with Bathsheba would die. This made David realize how grievous his sin really was.

I knew that I hadn't done anything like King David, but still, David was willing to repent and obey God and became a man after God's own heart. I knew that I was a sinner. Had I not confessed and repented? I couldn't help but feel that perhaps there was something in my life that displeased God, and as a result, my son Anzic was struck with these medical problems. This was causing me a lot of pain and anguish. Many nights I struggled with myself and examined my life from early on to the present, trying to understand how God would be so displeased with me that he would strike my son with such illness.

I realized I had countless sins and shortcomings, and I'd committed many errors in the choices I had made. I liked beautiful women just like David did, and I enjoyed looking at beautiful women wherever I went. Because of that, I'd had countless relationships and failed marriages. In those broken relationships, I had hurt many people—especially the women I became involved with, the men whom I stole the women from, and even their families. I know my wife also had many sleepless nights because of my fleshly desires, and she suspected my infidelity. Could this be God's punishment for all the broken relationships I was involved with before? Was it God's punishment for the pains I caused my wife? I knew I never cheated on my wife once we took our wedding vows. I'd been faithful, and I'd served our church with integrity and honor, making sure my life reflected what I preach. I was confused. Was there something I had overlooked?

I also examined my life for other possible causes for Anzic's condition. I looked at many events in my life where I might have displeased God. Some of these were small matters, but some were indeed life choices and paths that I took.

Was God punishing me for not choosing to become a pastor, as many had expected of me from my high school years? I remember in my elementary school years having a strong desire to attend Emmaus High School, a high school run by the Palau Evangelical Church and the only Christian high school for boys in the entire island. I had prepared myself by going to Sunday school and attending vacation Bible school each summer. I was familiar with most Sunday school teachers and Emmaus High School teachers. I was also familiar with most Bible stories by the time I entered high school. Since my knowledge of the Bible was apparent, and I served as unofficial spokesman for our class when it came to Bible or church-related activities, people often mentioned that I was destined to be a pastor. Most of my teachers and the pastors of our church spoke to me about becoming a pastor and serving God. I must admit that I really enjoy studying the Bible and discussing the Bible and church-related programs with fellow church workers. Even today, I have great joy and peace discussing biblical issues, perspectives, and their applications to everyday life.

So, did I disappoint God by choosing a different career path after college? To this day, I haven't been ordained a pastor. I feel that I should not be ordained unless I get a degree in some Bible-related field, which I believe to be a prerequisite for competent service that would inspire a church to follow the Lord truly and honestly. I felt that I failed that endeavor by not getting such a degree when I was young and living in the United States. Instead, I decided to go to law school, which I failed to complete.

Was God now punishing me for all this?

In my junior and senior years at Emmaus High School, we were privileged to carry out mission trips as part of our study of the book of Acts and Paul's missionary journeys. We went to outlying communities and visited people in their homes and shared God's Word with them. We also invited them to our services, which were held on Saturday evening and Sunday morning. Often, I was asked to share my testimony during the Saturday evening services, and on Sundays, I would run the service with the deacon or missionary assigned to that church. This gave me a lot of visibility in churches all over Palau at an early age. During these services, we were also encouraged by church leaders to consider entering into the ministry and work for God.

Perhaps many of the church members who saw me sharing my testimony and running programs felt that I'd already chosen to become a pastor. I was often told to be strong and to trust God and serve Him well. I was told that all these old folks would be gone someday, and I would be the only one left to run the church, since there appeared to be none more visible than I was.

Was God unhappy because my path did not follow what my high school teachers and church leaders predicted? Was God unhappy because I knew His Word but failed to make a commitment to full-time ministry? Was it all the women I'd been dating and sleeping around with? Was it my pride, since the Bible says pride comes before destruction? Did God want to use a disabled child to bring me to my knees?

Tears came to my eyes as I realized I'd taken too many wrong turns in my life, and especially my Christian journey.

I was still far from finding the answers I needed: the answer to my life and the answer to Anzic's illness. I felt so isolated, confused, and lost. Could God have abandoned me because of my sins, and now Anzic was paying the price for me? This was so painful, and I started to doubt if I would ever overcome such punishment.

King David later had several sons. But I expected that Anzic would be my only son, because of my age and also because my wife and I knew that having another child would not be a good idea.

Many questions came to my head. What we would do if Anzic turned out to be permanently disabled? What would become of him? What would become of this one brother to all my daughters?

My child's illness was draining my hope of having a normal son who would go fishing with me, go farming with me, and help me run errands. It was killing the hope of having a son who would be the strength and sole male heir to inherit the little resources I had and to provide brotherly help to his sisters. Instead, he might become a burden and a liability to them.

Did I really cause all this—because of my sins?

With all these things flowing through my mind that day in Shriner's Hospital, we reached the cafeteria and went on to order our food. As we sat down, Deacon Naito offered to pray. Before praying, he said, "Anzic is in better hands. Not only the hands of the doctors, but also in the hands of God." That reality struck me as I realized how helpless we are, and entrusting our children to God provides far more security than any other protection we offer. Deacon Naito prayed, and a sense of peace came over me. I knew that Anzic was in God's care at that time.

Anzic Kochi Alexander's early years photos

Anzic in his early years appeared as normal as any child. He started to show signs of disability at age two. Still, those very early years were very precious and wonderful memories. Now, we enjoy him for what he brings to us in his personality and spirit.

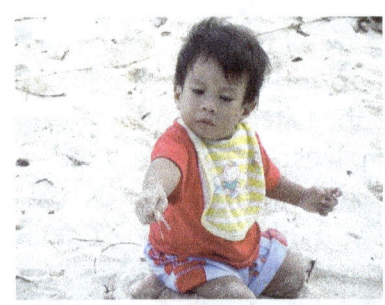

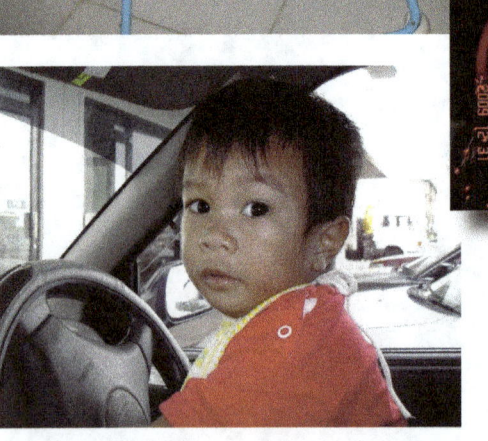

2

Anzic's Operation Throws a Curve Ball

At our lunch, we had barely finished our food when my wife's phone rang. All three of us froze. "Something has gone wrong!" I immediately thought. The operation was supposed to last at least four hours, and not even one hour had gone by.

My wife pressed the cell phone to her ear. I could hear the nurse clearly as she spoke.

"Mrs. Alexander?"

"Yes," my wife replied. My heart nearly stopped as I listened.

"Will you please go to the counseling room? The doctor would like to speak to you."

I immediately jumped out of my seat and was ready to move.

Deacon Naito said quietly, "This part is for the two of you, so I will wait in the lobby. Please let me know what's going on so I can inform the medical referral coordinator."

My wife said, "We will."

We bolted away, almost running down the hall. When we reached the elevator, I asked my wife what was wrong. She said she didn't know, that the nurse didn't say anything except that the doctor wanted to talk to us.

When we reached the counseling room, the doctor wasn't there. I checked to make sure we were in the right room. After a minute or two, when the doctor still didn't show up, I wanted to walk to the operating room to check with the doctor. My wife quietly urged me to be patient and wait. Although she, too, looked ready to panic, her voice was calm. She understood there was nothing we could do even if something had gone wrong. She said simply, "The doctor will come." I hesitantly sat down.

A couple of minutes later, the door opened. Dr. Moroz, the operating doctor for Anzic, came in and greeted us. I was able to breathe a sigh of relief. Dr. Moroz is a friendly man with an attitude that somehow was appealing to kids. Even Anzic wasn't afraid of him, but rather wanted to be with him.

Dr. Moroz wore somewhat of a smile on his face. He didn't look worried at all. He quickly assured us. "Anzic is fine," he said. "He's okay. We haven't operated on him yet." That quieted our nerves and enabled us to listen intently to what he was about to tell us.

He sat down and patiently explained that since he last looked at Anzic's x-ray, things seemed to have changed, and he wanted to be very sure before operating. Originally the bones that were fractured were close enough for a simple corrective operation. The plan had been that he would simply connect the two bones where they were fractured and brace them. However, now the bones seem to have shifted farther apart. Dr. Moroz told us that to avoid a larger incision and a huge scar afterward, it was imperative to bring in another doctor who was experienced in dealing with such a condition to avoid a big scar and future complications. He had a friend who was also an orthopedic surgeon and who had performed such surgeries. However, this doctor was currently on the island of Maui seeing his patients there. So, Dr. Moroz was seeking our permission to defer the operation and wait for his doctor friend to come and work alongside him in the procedure. Once again, he assured us that the operation should go smoothly and that we had nothing to worry about.

We realized that our fears were all for nothing. There was absolutely nothing to worry about, as the doctors really considered all parts of the operation for Anzic. They were looking for the best for him, even for the ease of the operation and the size of the scar afterward.

Since we knew little about the procedure, and had been reassured that everything was fine, we agreed. Anzic was brought back to the recovery room, and we joined him and waited for him to wake up. He was heavy-eyed and sleepy but was as happy to see us as we were to see him recover.

That evening we returned to the Shriners Hospital Family Center, where Anzic and my wife stayed. My wife's aunt, Debbie Shiro, called to find out about the surgery. My wife told her what had happened and explained that we would have to wait until the other doctor arrived from Maui.

Aunt Debbie invited us to take a ride around the island the next day, since she was off work. We felt that taking Anzic for a trip around the island would be good for him, especially after going through tests, sedation, x-rays, and so forth. A trip around the island, with a picnic to cap it off, would be good for him. We prepared snacks and drinks, and the next morning, Aunt Debbie came and picked us up for the trip. I was certain Anzic would enjoy the ride.

We first went to Dole Plantation Park, where we walked around and looked at gift shops, the gardens, and the birds. Anzic enjoyed himself. Next, we rode through the former plantation where there were still many plants—pineapple, sugar cane, coffee trees, and more. I put Anzic on my lap to help give him a better view outside. He had a calm and peaceful expression as he enjoyed the scenery. At one moment I thought, "Was it only yesterday he was supposed to be operated on? He was supposed to be in a cast now! Yet here he is enjoying himself." What joy that gave me. I sensed the upcoming operation would give Anzic more life—not that it would make him walk, but that it would ease his pain and allow him to move with ease.

I kept going back to Jesus and what he would do, if he was present with us, for Anzic. I guess I was trying to figure out the Lord's thinking and possible plans for Anzic. I kept struggling with the idea that Anzic had a special place in

God's plan. And one of the things coming to mind was that if Jesus was here with us, healing Anzic would be a great testimony and would bring glory to God. Then I realized that God is omnipresent. Jesus said He and the Father are one and the same. So, in all honesty, Jesus *was* here. He was right there with us. So, what was he going to do about Anzic? What *could* He do for him—and would he do it? What did I need to do to get him to do something for poor Anzic? Did I need to get down on my knees and beg and plead until something happened?

I was reminded of the story of Jesus and the centurion whose servant was very sick, a story told in Luke 7:1-10. Although this centurion was a Gentile, he'd heard of Jesus and the great things he was doing. He probably wondered if this prophet of the Jews would have anything to do with him. But because he understood authority, he was also well aware of the authority Jesus had. So, when his highly valued servant became sick, he sought out Jesus's help.

The story tells clearly of two things. First, it tells us about ourselves and how unworthy we are to come before God. The centurion himself didn't go to Jesus but sent elders of the Jews to plead with Jesus for his servant. When Jesus agreed to go and heal the servant, the centurion sent other messengers to stop Jesus and begged him to use his authority without going to the centurion's house, for he felt unworthy.

I also felt so unworthy at this point. I felt like Anzic's illness and his suffering were a result of my doing. I was a sinful man with sinful intentions, and they were bringing ruin to our lives. I felt so ashamed that I couldn't ask God to heal Anzic. I'd done so many wrongs in my life. But the encouragement of my deacon colleagues and the pastors gave me the courage to plead with God for Anzic's sake.

I could identify with the centurion. Seeing Anzic suffer just made me want to cry out to Jesus. I knew Jesus had authority to heal my son, and I wished He would appear and make him well. I wished He would come, so I could beg for Anzic to be healed.

The second thing this story tells us is that Jesus is willing to heal, restore, and redeem those with ailments. This isn't based on our status or standing or whether we've lived a holy life. This centurion was a Gentile, and his servant was probably a Gentile as well. They weren't among the chosen people. Jesus was pleased with the man's faith just as he was pleased with the Canaanite woman's faith and healed her daughter (Matthew 15:21-28). Similarly, he was willing to go to the centurion's house to heal his servant, but when the centurion sent other messengers to tell him he was unworthy for Jesus to go to his house, Jesus was amazed with the man's faith.

I began to wonder if I had faith — faith like the centurion's faith, or like the Canaanite woman's faith. Was it because I didn't have faith that Anzic had not been healed? I knew that Jesus was ready to heal and help Anzic. So, what kept him from doing so? I kept wondering as we drove around Oahu on our tour with Aunt Debbie.

I believe those two stories — about the centurion pleading for his servant, and the Canaanite woman pleading for her daughter — give very important lessons to the followers of Jesus. I don't believe Jesus really meant for a group of people to be identified with dogs (Matthew 15:26-27). If they were, all who are Gentiles today have no real hope in God's salvation.

I believe the lesson of the story about the Canaanite woman was to demonstrate that even those seen by the people of Israel as Gentiles are capable of having faith in the Son of God. Having such faith enables one to believe that God is fair and shares his grace and blessings even with Gentiles.

The centurion believed that God would provide healing for his servant just as he did for the Jews. Jesus demonstrated that grace will be extended to anyone who believes, confirming his message of John 3:16 — "For God so loved the world that He gave His only Son, that whoever [anyone: Jew or Gentile] believes in him will not perish but will have eternal life."

This gave me a bit of comfort, knowing that God doesn't discriminate based on our status, our position, or even our cleanliness. He extends grace because He chooses to and because He is love. We have to trust him and believe in what he can do.

I knew then that Anzic would be all right. Even if he would never walk, I knew that he would be in Jesus's grace and care and would receive blessings from Him. I wondered how God would use Anzic. What could Anzic do to demonstrate God's love for him and people like him? He looked so fragile and was in constant need of someone to help him.

But right now, as we rode along, he was calm. Looking out the car window, he had such a peaceful look on his face, as from a heart filled and overflowing with joy.

As we went through the old Dole Plantation, I was at peace, hoping it would always be like this. I gave my son a squeeze and a gentle hug.

As we drove by rows and rows of pineapple, he seemed to enjoy the scenery. Once in a while he would say something and point out the window toward the pineapple plants, the hills in the background, and the random houses' we passed along the way. He would speak with excitement and point out the window and smile, as though saying, "I like that." I remember wishing it would always be like that for him. Here was a boy who all his life might never experience working on a farm by planting seeds or tilling a field. He would always be a bystander. So, this moment was a special one for both of us. I felt that God was enabling us to enjoy His creation together, even if we were mere observers.

Then we went to the Northshore Park. After we found a parking space, we went out and looked for a picnic table to occupy. We were fortunate to find one under a huge tree, which provided shade and also a little privacy from the sunbathers nearby. We unloaded our lunch boxes and a cooler with drinks and brought them to our newly claimed picnic area. My wife and Aunt Debbie prepared lunch, and we ate and talked.

We all believed that it was God's grace that we brought Anzic to the park, so he could enjoy a little bit of outdoors before going in for the big surgery. My wife said that she and Anzic could have easily been stuck at Shriners Hospital at this time if the surgery had gone ahead. He would be lying on his back with a heavy cast on his legs and lower belly, while she would be busy taking care of him. This was a good opportunity and a blessing for both of them to be outside and to enjoy Hawaii before being tied down with the cast and bandages.

Anzic started to make noise and notified us that he wanted to take a look around the park. I pushed him around in his wheelchair as gently as I could over the bumpy, uneven ground. We went near the water and looked at the swimmers. He wanted to move closer, but the wheels on his wheelchair wouldn't move in the sand. So, we strolled around for a while on the small sidewalk as Anzic pointed to areas he wanted to explore. Although it was hot, I really enjoyed this time with Anzic. When people walked by, he would always say, "Hi." People would respond by saying "Hi" back. He seemed to like that. He didn't seem to realize that he was disabled and had limited mobility, unlike the others. He took the opportunity to enjoy what was made available to him and what was given to him. His cheerful spirit gave me great joy as I watched him greet everyone and smile widely when people responded back to him. I was very happy to see him happy.

We stayed in the park for about three hours. Then we packed up and started our long journey back to Honolulu. Once inside the car, I decided to lift him up and put him on my lap again so he could watch the scenery on our return trip. I had to put my seat belt around us both as we rode together. On the way back, we attempted to try a famous shrimp restaurant we'd heard of. It was situated in the middle of what appeared to be a small park with tents, benches, and some chairs for customers. When we pulled in, we couldn't find any parking. It appeared that many people had heard of this place and their famous shrimp. Because it was so crowded, we decided to head back to Honolulu.

As we were pulling out of the parking lot, Anzic started to move uneasily. All of a sudden, he started yanking the seat belt crying for me to take it off. I quickly took it off and slowly took him from my lap and sat him on the seat cushioned with a pillow. He became quiet and seemed to relax. I thought perhaps he was uncomfortable sitting on my lap, so I settled him next to me in the back. I put on his seat belt, and we began to move again.

After about twenty minutes he was pulling the seat belt again, this time crying with anger and frustration. It seemed as though something was irritating him or causing him a great deal of discomfort. I quickly unbuckled his seat belt. Almost immediately, he started pulling at the waistband of his pants. Since Anzic couldn't talk, I had no clue what was happening, but he seemed to be in serious pain. We stopped the car, and my wife jumped out and came to the back. She asked Anzic if he was hurting, and he nodded. She asked if he wanted her to change him, and he gave an angry, negative response. She then asked if he wanted his bottle (Anzic still used a bottle to eat). But he also responded angrily to this.

We took off his pants and his pampers and covered him with a *lavlav*, a piece of cloth that looked like a colorful towel. By this time, it was obvious Anzic was in severe pain.

Aunt Debbie, being very thoughtful, decided to cancel the rest of the trip and return immediately to Honolulu, which was a long forty-minute ride back. By the time we reached Shriners Hospital, Anzic didn't want to be touched and didn't want us to move him. I slowly put him in his wheelchair and wheeled him toward our room. He fought me every step of the way, especially when he realized I was trying to get him to our room. My wife and I pleaded with him. It took another thirty minutes before he finally agreed to go to the room. We quickly removed his clothing and tried to shower him.

It was then that we noticed that his lower parts were starting to swell. We quickly showered him, hoping that once clean, and after a brief rest, he might feel better. We clothed him and tried to put him to sleep for a brief nap, but he couldn't sleep. Instead, he began to turn red in the face and to perspire profusely. My wife and I ached and cried inside when we realized how much pain he was in.

We called the Shriners Hospital pediatrician. This doctor came quickly and looked at Anzic. When we took off his clothes and his pampers, the swelling had increased. His testicles looked much bigger than when we'd put on his clothes only a few minutes earlier. The expression on the doctor's face told us that this was an emergency. He told us to take Anzic to a hospital across the street from Shriners Hospital. This was the Kapi'olani Medical Center for Women and Children. My wife quietly told him, "Doctor, we don't have insurance." We knew if we went to Kapi'olani, we would need to have insurance or else bear the entire cost.

The doctor told us to wait. As he made a phone call, we tried to calm Anzic. After the call, the doctor told us that in his opinion we had to bring Anzic to the emergency room immediately. My wife reminded him again that we didn't have any insurance. The pediatrician said we would worry about that later, but now Anzic was in great pain, and we had to take him there. He volunteered to call the ambulance for Anzic. When we told him we could take Anzic there in his wheelchair, he told us simply, "Go now."

When we told Anzic we were going to the hospital, he nodded. He looked as though this was what he wanted in the first place, and we just hadn't understood him. I considered the situation and felt that in his condition, anything to relieve pain was welcome.

The pediatrician called the Kapi'olani emergency room and told them we were coming with a patient named Anzic Alexander, who was a patient at Shriners Hospital. He apparently told them how serious his condition was and that he had to be seen right away.

We wheeled Anzic across Punahou Street and into Kapi'olani Medical Center. When we arrived, the emergency room was crowded with children and women waiting to be called. "Oh, great," I thought, "these are all emergency cases. We'll have to wait in line." So, we went and registered, and were asked if this was our first time there. We answered yes. We were told that a chart must be prepared for Anzic, which would take a while. My heart sank further, since Anzic was now grimacing from the discomfort of the short trip across the street from Shriners Hospital. Even the other patients saw that he was in agony.

There were no vacant seats in the room, so we stood by the main door, unsure of where to go. A family with many children saw our dilemma, and the woman asked her two children, who apparently were just accompanying them there, to give us their chairs. We graciously thanked them and went and sat down. Almost as soon as we did so, the nurse came out and called for Anzic. My wife quietly said that it must have been information from the Shriners Hospital pediatrician that caused them to take us before all these people who were waiting. Nonetheless, God must have seen Anzic in pain, and knowing his sufferings, He arranged for Anzic to go before the others.

Jesus once said, "Bring the children to me, for theirs is the kingdom of heaven." This shows the heart of our Lord Jesus Christ when it comes to children. He gives them highest regard. In Matthew 18, Jesus told his disciples, "I tell you the truth, unless you become like this little child, you will never enter into the kingdom of God. Therefore, whoever humbles himself like this little child is the greatest in the kingdom of God." Children are humble enough to know their place and to honor, respect, and accept the guidance of elders. Anzic is no different. It's his willingness to accept what's being done or given to him, even when he doesn't like it, that makes him so admirable. When he's made to understand that he must do or take something, he'll do or take it.

I realized that God must have been preparing Anzic for this very treatment. He must have known well ahead of time that Anzic's condition would require a very serious surgical intervention and prepared his heart and mind to be as accepting as possible. It gives me great peace of mind that God is fully prepared for any situation we enter. He has already planned out what His intervention will be before we even ask. This shows how loving and gracious our God is.

Anzic Kochi Alexander, age two, as he started to grow

Anzic Alexander has always had a friendly, outgoing personality. He appeared to be intrigued by other people and what was happening around him. He enjoyed going outside, attending church programs, and even joining the quarterly Youth Conference of the Palau Evangelical Church as shown directly below.

3

God Gives Anzic a Better Treatment

Anzic didn't fight the treatment or the people administering the treatment at the Kapi'olani emergency care area. He showed signs of discomfort, pain, and suffering, but he also showed courage and willingness to accept the painful treatment that was offered.

In the examination area, a nurse came quickly and took Anzic's vital signs—blood pressure, temperature, a quick look at his eyes and mouth, and so forth. A doctor came and looked at Anzic, then said that they would need to run some tests. Laboratory technicians came and took blood samples and urine samples. We were also told that Anzic needed to have an ultrasound. This was all happening so fast that we were like bystanders watching a movie in fast-forward.

Anzic's testicles had continued to swell, and his pain increased. When the tests came back, they showed symptoms of serious infection in the lower part of his body, from his navel down to his scrotum. What was puzzling was that they hadn't been able to find the cause of the infection. So, they asked if we would give permission for a CT scan to be taken. There were risks for Anzic with this test, due to the high radiation levels, but we were told it had to be done in order to identify the source of this infection.

Their concern was increased by the fact that this wasn't the first time he'd had a similar infection. Back in Palau, the doctors had been puzzled with these frequent scrotum infections in Anzic, but they treated only the symptoms and never bothered to try and locate the source. It seemed like he would be hospitalized for infection every other week. We knew that the hospital in Palau was limited in resources, expertise, and proper equipment, so we weren't surprised that they weren't able to locate the source of the infection.

We gave our permission for the CT scan at Kapi'olani. After the scan, Anzic was admitted to the hospital's Intensive Care Unit (ICU) for observation while we waited for a urologist to read the scan and determine a diagnosis. My wife and I took turns watching him in the ICU. His condition started to improve as they gave him a number of antibiotics to treat the infection.

After the urologist, Dr. Sutherland, looked at his CT scan results, he informed us that he saw a dark spot near the bladder, but was unsure what it was. Unfortunately, the CT scan wasn't able to produce a clearer picture to diagnose Anzic's problem. He asked permission to do an MRI, which had a much higher resolution with more details and would give a better view and understanding of what was ailing our son. But it would have a much higher risk, since it involved substantial radiation for such a young boy. Dr. Sutherland told us that unless the cause of the infection was found, Anzic might have problems with the hip surgery. In his professional opinion, this had to be taken care of first before the surgery. In our hearts we felt that he was absolutely right, so we signed the permission papers for the MRI scan.

Dr. Sutherland assured us by telling us he'd been to Palau a number of times, as he used to be the head of the urology program at Tripler Army Medical Center and occasionally visited Palau in his work. He had many patients from Palau, Guam, Federated States of Micronesia, and the Republic of the Marshall Islands. He operated on persons of all ages, including children. So, for him, Anzic's case was like going back to the islands. He appeared to take a special liking toward Anzic and asked if we would agree that he would be his doctor once we found out what the dark spot was and what was making him sick all the time.

He also told us that he was quite disturbed by our son's record of numerous admissions in Palau for infection of the scrotum, and yet he was never referred to the urology team that visits the island twice a year. He told us that he really wanted to help Anzic, since he saw that he was in such great pain.

Dr. Sutherland was very caring and straightforward in addressing us and appeared to genuinely care for Anzic. We took a special liking to him, as well as to all the doctors and nurses at Kapi'olani. They showed such professionalism and loving care. God certainly had laid out a wonderful treatment plan for Anzic with such professional people in a very capable hospital.

Dr. Sutherland, very highly regarded in his field, committed himself to treating Anzic. He took time to care for Anzic as his personal physician when he didn't have to. This gave us great comfort that Anzic was cared for at the highest level in the field of urology. Both my wife and I were so touched by Dr. Sutherland's commitment to help Anzic. We both realized that this is how our God works when we turn things over to him. He gives us the very best.

My wife and I felt the love of God shining through Anzic and all the people who cared for him. We felt so much closer to God, and we felt God was directly intervening in his life. Anzic's life appeared to consist of one miracle after another. It reminded us so much of how God still intervenes for us in this present age.

We're told in Psalm 39:11, "The LORD gives strength to his people; The LORD blesses his people with peace." As this verse came to mind, it gave me so much confidence that God is always with us, and this was clearly demonstrated in how people cared for Anzic. They had such peace, although Anzic had a myriad of challenges to be dealt with.

I was left speechless by God's grace. I wondered why we so often overlook God's loving kindness and seek to pursue worldly things, hoping they'll make our lives better. The result is only ruin. Yet God lovingly cares for us and blesses us each day of our lives without prejudice. He never holds our past sins against us once they're confessed.

I was comforted and reassured that God was in control of everything. He was going to heal Anzic in the best way possible. I recalled that when we left Palau, the doctors and nurses had told us, "Please ask the people at Shriners Hospital to find out why Anzic gets these infections. Please ask them to cure him so that when he returns, he doesn't spend so much time in the hospital." I sensed that God was addressing this request now, knowing that it came not only from the hospital in Palau but also from my wife and me. We longed to have Anzic overcome the infections so he could move forward with the treatment for his bones.

At this point, Dr. Sutherland told us he would get back to us as soon as he looked at the MRI results. The next day, we prepared Anzic for the MRI scan. I'd heard that patients often freak out when going into the MRI tube. I had some fear for Anzic, since an acquaintance of mine had supposedly died from fear when he was inserted into the MRI machine.

As we wheeled Anzic into the MRI room, he started to show signs of panic and great anxiety. Apparently, the doctors taking his MRI scan anticipated such a reaction and were prepared to deliver anesthesia. They quickly put Anzic to sleep to relieve him of the fear of the loud MRI machine, and also to ensure that the scan wasn't compromised by his movements and resistance.

About an hour later, I rejoined Anzic in the recovery room and waited for him to wake up. When he woke, he was scared at first, but then calmed down and was able to close his eyes in a relaxed manner.

A couple of hours later, we were with Anzic in his hospital room when Dr. Sutherland came in to report on the MRI results. He said it appeared to show a mass of scarred tissue behind the bladder — between the bladder and Anzic's back. This scarred tissue looked like a cyst which was approximately two and a half inches long. This was rather large for a cyst, and it would have to be removed immediately. It was

God Gives Anzic a Better Treatment 31

apparently the host for the infecting bacteria, having fluid inside that was sealed with tissue. The previous treatment of antibiotics killed the bacteria only in Anzic's bloodstream and urinary tract, but not inside the cyst. As soon as the bacteria in the bloodstream died, Anzic would feel better. However, when he was taken off antibiotics, the bacteria would come out of the cyst and infect him again. That was why he was hospitalized almost every other week in Palau for scrotum infections.

Dr. Sutherland told us that we were lucky Anzic didn't have the hip surgery as earlier scheduled. If he'd had the surgery, and the infection then reoccurred, there would have been dire consequences. He informed us that he would consult with Dr. Moroz of Shriners Hospital, because he felt very strongly that the operation to remove the cyst should take precedence over the hip surgery for Anzic's safety and care.

At that moment, we realized that God had a hand in all this. The prioritizing of the operations for Anzic was planned by God. He made sure Anzic's scheduled operations at Shriners Hospital were postponed so that this ongoing medical problem with Anzic could be addressed first. We were so humbled, because we realized that God was responding in an amazing way to the prayers from our family members and friends. We agreed with Dr. Sutherland that he should talk to Dr. Moroz.

The next day, a social worker came and told us that Shriners Hospital had kindly agreed that Anzic should have the cyst surgery first, and that Shriners would treat him after full recovery from the cyst surgery. She also told us that Dr. Sutherland wanted to schedule the cyst surgery right away, if we had no objections. We didn't.

The following day, we were told the surgery had been scheduled. Dr. Sutherland came and explained the surgery to us and asked if it was okay with us if he took the lead in the surgery. Having seen his concern for Anzic and his caring character, we were more than happy to have him do the surgery. Once everything was set, we were so happy that the recurring issue of infection would finally be taken care of. We praised God for all that He had done so far for Anzic and for us.

It all became very clear to both my wife and me. It was God who caused Anzic's bones to shift so the hip surgery could be stopped. It was God who caused Dr. Moroz's friend to be out of Oahu so the new schedule would be extended until he returned. It was God who caused my wife's aunt to be so free that she could take us for a trip around the island. It was God who caused the severe infection on Anzic so that we would have no choice but to bring him to Kapi'olani Medical Center for treatment. It was God who brought in Dr. Sutherland—a highly respected doctor in his field and quite well known throughout the region—to treat Anzic in this very delicate situation. It was all now very clear: God had been busy at work this whole time. He had answered our prayer to heal Anzic so he didn't get infected again.

The First Surgery and Recovery photos, 2012 in Honolulu, Hawaii

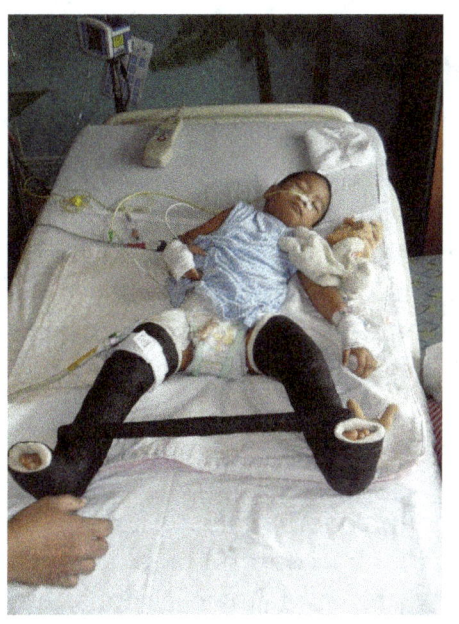

The first surgery to correct the hip joints. The femur bones were both broken and bent to fit into the hip bone and then secured so that he does not dislodge the joint. He remained in this position for nearly six weeks. My beautiful wife patiently took care of him during this time. They both had a number of visitors who went to visit them at the hospital.

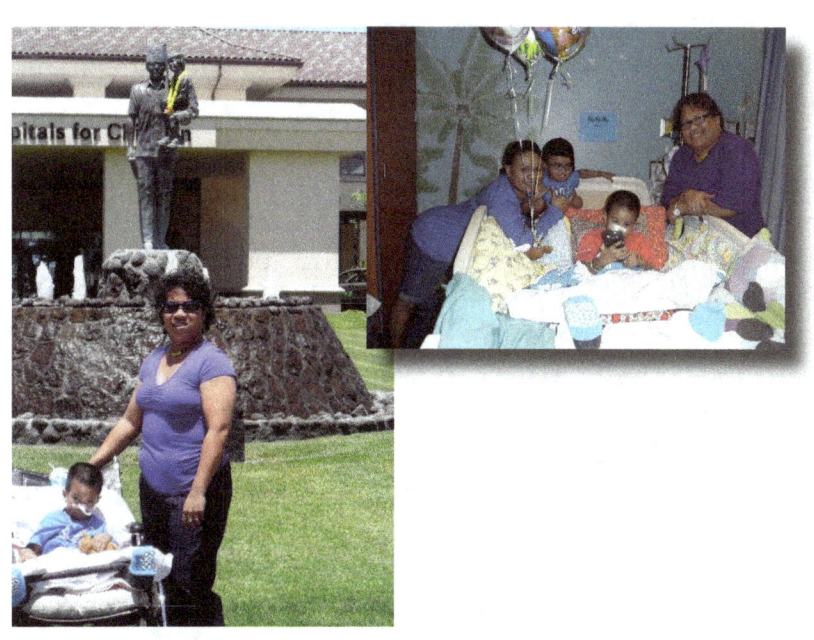

4

The Surgery Is Postponed Yet Again

Two days later—and only two days before Anzic's scheduled surgery to remove the cyst—the financial office at Kapi'olani Medical Center informed us that because we didn't have insurance, they could not approve the surgery. Further, we would have to leave the hospital immediately for liability reasons.

This announcement deflated both my wife and I. Anzic, oblivious to all this, seemed to be in good spirits, since he'd started to feel better from the infection attack. But my wife and I were so down in spirit that we couldn't talk, not even to each other. My wife quietly prepared Anzic's things, and we packed our belongings and prepared to leave. It felt like an eviction, or even a rejection. I really wanted to scream, and I felt like such a failure, since I'd been unable to secure insurance for us so that my son wouldn't have to delay his surgery.

The hospital nurses and support staff were also at a loss for words, as they realized our son wasn't going to get this most needed treatment but would be released out to the community where we would have to fend for ourselves. They told us to get all the diapers that were there in our room, the underpads, the rubber gloves—whatever was there, they offered to us. I knew it was out of sympathy that they were extra nice to us. It felt good to have so many people paying attention to us and especially to Anzic.

In my heart, I was crying out to God: "What's the meaning of this? Where are you leading us?" Again, my thoughts turned to questions that had bothered me before: Was it sin in our lives that was causing Anzic's treatment to be halted?

I had many questions running through my head yet again. Meanwhile, my wife didn't say much, but quietly went about the business of getting ready for the discharge.

Dr. Sutherland came in to pay us a last visit. He advised us that he would prescribe medicine to take care of the bacteria and that Anzic was to take it until the cyst was removed, however long that took. The doctor didn't blame us for the insurance problems, and genuinely sought ways to make sure Anzic was safe and protected. He prescribed the antibiotic for sixty days. We took this as a sign that God would provide a way for Anzic to have the cyst surgery within sixty days.

Soon after Dr. Sutherland left, the social worker came and told us that we needed to go down to the hospital's administration and finance office to sign the release papers before departing the hospital. When we went down to this office, we were advised that Shriners Hospital had declined paying for Anzic's care at the Kapi'olani Medical Center. The Kapi'olani administration had assumed (as we had) that Shriners Hospital would bear the cost; these two medical institutions had been partners for a long time, and when they refer patients, they often pay for the cost. So, it was surprising when Shriners Hospital decided not to cover Anzic's treatment.

They presumed correctly that we didn't have the financial means to cover the hospital cost there. We didn't know what to say, as we, too, had counted on Shriners Hospital to cover the cost, at the emergency room at least. Since it was a Shriners doctor, the pediatrician, who advised us to take Anzic to the emergency room at the Kapi'olani Medical Center, we felt they should at least help with the cost.

We weren't angry, as we knew the Kapi'olani personnel had tried their best to save Anzic. If he didn't have the treatment he'd received, he might have died. We would have been helpless to protect him. So at least he was saved by the emergency treatment at Kapi'olani Medical Center. But we looked to see where God was leading us. Meanwhile, our spirits were so downcast that even praying was hard. My wife and I simply leaned on God and cried out in our hearts, not knowing what to do.

God knew what to do, and amazingly, He had it planned all along. In our limited faith, we didn't see that. But when things began to unfold, we realized once again that He had a far better plan than any we knew.

It started with the financial officer telling us we had to apply to Med-QUEST (Hawaii's state-run Medicaid coverage agency) for financial assistance to cover the time Anzic had been admitted to the hospital and to include the needed surgery. Our hearts were lifted. But then she said that Med-QUEST is for Hawaii residents, so we might not qualify, though we needed to try. Our hearts sank again. We took the application, and we went back to the Shriners Hospital Family Center.

Both my wife and I sensed that a piece of the puzzle was missing. What was it? We went over the events leading to Anzic going to Kapi'olani Medical Center and agreed that it was the pediatrician who advised us to take Anzic there. Why wouldn't Shriners Hospital agree to pay for the emergency and the surgery? We weren't trying to blame anyone; we were trying to find out where God was leading us. However, we felt like we were pointing fingers, so we immediately stopped, and we prayed.

We got on our knees and begged God for forgiveness and guidance. We felt strongly that this was not the time to point fingers at anyone but a time to find out where God was leading in providing treatment for Anzic as well as healing our spiritual blindness. The doctors, staff, and workers of both hospitals had been more than generous to us with their compassion and care, and we were extremely grateful. We knew God was waiting to demonstrate another miracle to make sure Anzic would have this much-needed surgery. So, while we were depressed, we were not hopeless.

The next day we completed the application form for Med-QUEST and brought it to the financial office at Kapi'olani Medical Center. They reviewed the form and gave us a few tips on how to present the application to Med-QUEST and told us we should take it personally to their office that same day. My wife called the Palau government's medical referral office (called *Blai er a Omekungil,* translated as "House of Healing") and talked with Ms. Allyn Takada Naito, the medical coordinator (and wife of Deacon Uchel Naito). My wife asked if we could be assisted to bring the application to Med-QUEST. We were immediately given approval for one of their drivers to come and give us a ride to Med-QUEST.

We went back to the Shriners Hospital Family Center and called our daughters. Thankfully, one of them was free to watch Anzic while we went away.

When we entered the Med-QUEST office, we saw many people there applying for Med-QUEST. We told the receptionist that we wanted to see a counselor. She told us to leave our completed application, and they would give us a call.

At the financial office at Kapi'olani Medical Center, we were told to make sure we talked to a counselor at Med-QUEST and explained our situation, since we were not local residents. So, I insisted on seeing a counselor. We were told there were no counselors in the office. So, I told them we would wait for one to come. We saw a number of people being called in to talk to someone. So, we took a number and sat down. After quite a while, I went up to the counter to find out if and when our turn would come up. The young lady told me matter-of-factly that we would not be seeing a counselor, but she nicely asked what we wanted to talk to the counselor about. I quickly explained our dilemma and why we were there.

She looked at our application and saw that we had listed the Shriners Hospital address as our address. She told us that this hospital provided free services for children and asked why we were asking for support. We told her that our son had gone for medical treatment at Kapi'olani Medical Center across the street. After we explained our situation, she said it appeared that we were not residents, and that the Med-QUEST program was for local residents, which is the main criteria for qualification. We were speechless, because she was right. We were not local residents. Our hearts sank yet again.

The young lady apparently saw our concerned faces and quickly said, "I'll go ahead and bring it to the committee, but I just wanted to let you know." She then looked more closely at the application and said, "The committee members won't understand why patients at a free hospital are asking for financial support, and they may deny your application." She offered a suggestion: "Why don't you find someone here in Hawaii whose address you can use instead of the address for Shriners Hospital. Then we'll just have to pray that they overlook the fact that you're not local residents, and that they approve your request."

My wife and I exchanged looks, as we immediately sought an address we could use. The young lady at Med-QUEST further suggested that we use an address that would immediately bring any reply to our attention, because any response would come only via regular mail and not email. My wife quickly looked at me and mentioned that Allyn of the Palau Medical Referral Office told her that if any needed mail could be sent to her office. So, we decided to use the address of the Palau Medical Referral Office.

After we changed the address, the young lady looked at our application one more time and smiled. She told us, "No promises, but I'll give it to the committee, and let's hope for the best." We kindly thanked her for her help and for her willingness to take our application to the committee, and we left.

When we came out, the driver was nowhere in sight, so we decided to eat lunch while we waited. This was the first time my wife and I were by ourselves, away from Anzic and the busy life he puts us through, as well as away from the hustle of trying to find ways to care for him. So, we tried to gather our thoughts and share ideas about what had happened. We both agreed that the situation was clearly out of our hands and that God was leading Anzic's medical treatment down a path that was out of our control. We agreed to simply trust God and follow His lead. We bowed our heads and simply told God that we knew He had a plan both for us and for our son, that we knew He was in control, and that we were willing to follow Him.

Somehow, we felt at peace as never before. Our state was peaceful enough that we felt hungry. We realized that we hadn't eaten a regular meal for a day or two. We saw a sign for a restaurant in the building next to the Med-QUEST building, so we headed there. Since we didn't see the driver, we sat down and ordered our food.

When our food arrived, I prepared to pray and was reminded of the words of Jesus in John 14:27 where He says, "Peace I leave with you; my peace I give to you. I do not give to you as the world gives. Do not let your hearts be troubled and do not be afraid." As we prayed, we felt a strong sense of assurance that God would take care of everything.

The driver was actually already parked outside in the parking lot. He even saw us come out of the building but didn't try to contact us. The parking lot was big, so we didn't notice him being there. He sent us a text message which we received in the middle of our lunch and said that he would wait until we finished. We immediately asked for take-out containers and paid our bill and went out.

It was a good thing that we left right at that time. Once we were in the car, our daughter texted us to say that Anzic was in one of his destructive moods, which usually meant that he wasn't afraid of the babysitter and wanted to challenge that person's authority over him.

We reached the Shriners Hospital Family Center to find our daughter Ja-el (whom we call O.B.) about ready to pull her hair out.   Anzic was in his happy mood, thinking he could do whatever he wanted because his parents were both gone. When he didn't get the attention he wanted from O.B. — because she was trying to do some studies — he would try to tear apart whatever he could get his hands on. He had thrown the contents of a drawer onto the floor, and when O.B. went to clean it up, he threw food items on the floor. O.B. had given up cleaning his mess and decided to wait for us. This gave Anzic the thrill of seeing that he was getting on someone's nerves. O.B. was clearly and visibly upset with him. I'm not sure whether Anzic enjoyed the attention (even if it was very angry attention), or simply the fact that she was now very annoyed by his behavior.

They were both happy to see us. Anzic immediately asked me to take him outside to get away from Mom, because she was now angry that he'd made a big mess. O.B. was happy to be relieved of her babysitting duties.

So Anzic and I escaped for a walk. There's something about Anzic that just makes me very weak in my discipline, and I tend to let him get away with most things (I know that this isn't because he's a disabled person, but rather because he emanates innocence). That day, it was like, "Hey, everything is fine and cool, and I'm simply asking you to take me for a walk."

Anzic's disability and limitations make him enjoy every opportunity to be pushed out of the room and out into the open area. He enjoys a simple push around the parking lot to look at parked cars or sitting still on the sidewalk and watching passing vehicles. He gets excited when an old car, mostly an old sedan, is passing by. Somehow, he likes old cars and prefers little toy cars that replicate old style sedans. It made me sad and yet happy at the same time to see him so happy.

As his father, I was sad knowing Anzic had so many limitations and might never be able to enjoy some things in life that other people consider important. Once again, I thought through what he would miss: farming, fishing, playing ball, and swinging independently. He might never be able to enjoy intimacy with a wife, and to have children and head a family, and to enjoy caring, guiding, and rearing children. He might never celebrate a wedding anniversary or a child's birthday, or attend graduation to congratulate his children, nor be able to walk anyone down an aisle on their wedding.

Further, he might never be able to play any sports. He might always be a child looking for attention and for someone to help him get around. But he would enjoy loud noises like that of cars, carnivals, theme parks, and leisure rides around the countryside or even in the city.

As I pushed Anzic around the parking lot of Shriners Hospital, I started to think about his early years and how much he had already missed in life.

Recovery photos at the hospital in Hawaii and at home on the Beach near his sister's high school, Bethania High School (2012).

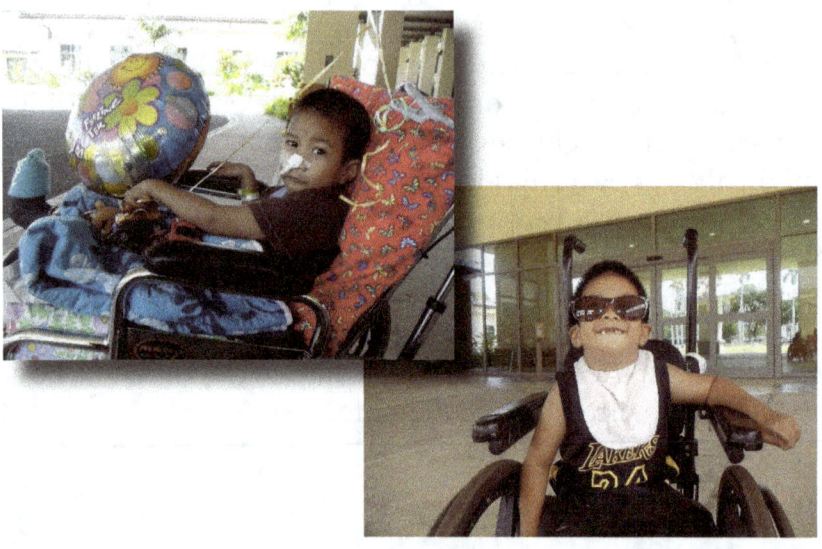

Anzic Alexander recovering at the Shriner hospital in Hawaii. Upon completion of the treatment, he returned home to his most enjoyable activities, playing on the beach, catching hermit crab, and rafting. Anzic could not swim as he is unable to use his legs fully.

5

Anzic's Early Years

When we first realized that Anzic possibly had medical challenges, I was always of the belief that there was a cure. I always felt that medicine nowadays was so advanced that doctors can treat anything except death. So, I wasn't really too concerned about Anzic, as I always felt, perhaps hoped, that things would be all right in the end and Anzic would become a normal child.

Anzic was about three years old when he had his first surgery, to relieve a hernia that he'd had for a while but wasn't detected. During that time, I asked the doctors to assess why Anzic wasn't walking yet. We were always told that some kids take longer to learn to walk, and we should give him time and not push him. So, we had. We simply kept hoping. Since the doctors were going to operate on him for the hernia, perhaps they could find out the reason he couldn't walk. However, we were told yet again that only time could heal this late development.

Anzic was four years old when he had his second hernia surgery. By then, I was really concerned why he wasn't walking or eating properly. My daughters Balie and O.B. were also very concerned. Balie, the oldest daughter, found some information on the internet and informed us that Anzic might have cerebral palsy. I thought, "No way." But as the days went by, I began to pay close attention to his abilities, movements, and behaviors, and I began to wonder if Balie was right. I asked her for more information about cerebral palsy. She printed out some information from the internet and gave this to me.

From what I read, it sounded pretty much like she was

right. She'd been observing Anzic, and she felt that his behavior, challenges, and movements matched with conditions associated with cerebral palsy. I concluded that my son probably had cerebral palsy. However, because it was never confirmed by a doctor, I kept telling myself that he didn't have cerebral palsy and that he was normal.

Because we all were hopeful for Anzic's development, and because of what the doctors kept telling us, we never really paid attention to his special needs, and more importantly, his wants. We began to notice that he seemed content to simply crawl around the house or to be carried around by someone, which most often was me, and not bother even to try to walk. We also noticed that he liked toy cars more than anything, especially small toy cars. He had a favorite stuffed doggie, but he really didn't care much about anything else.

When Anzic was five years old, he was included in the program to receive care from the visiting Shriners Hospital medical team. In our first ever visit with them, the doctor asked for x-rays and examined Anzic very carefully, then sat down to talk to us. He told us that in order to fix Anzic's legs to give him a chance to walk, he would have to take him to Hawaii to Shriners Hospital, where they have better equipment, and then he would have to fix him there. He told us that because Anzic hadn't used his legs for a long time, the bones were weak. But there was another problem that was much worse, and he told us about the problem with Anzic sitting in a W position instead of cross-legged, and how this had separated the hip joint from the leg bone to a distance that his leg bones weren't supporting his weight.

The doctor also told us that in this situation, as Anzic grew older, there would be constant pain because of the femur bones not being in their right place. The hip joint would most likely fill with fat or tissue, creating discomfort, and the bones would be pressing against the muscles, creating pain every time he moved or pressure was put on his legs. He needed corrective surgery to try and get the bones in their right place and, hopefully, give Anzic a chance to walk and also to relieve him of pain.

The doctor wanted us to go home and think all this over, then tell the local Palau doctors what we decided.

It required some deep consideration before we could decide. The doctor told us that the treatment would require them to break the femur bone on both legs just below the tip of the bone, just a few inches below the ball that goes into the hip joint. They would insert the ball into the hip joint and hold it with a bolt, then connect the broken bone at an angle and brace it with hardware that would have to come out after the bone healed. The thought of breaking Anzic's bones was shocking to us; it gave both my wife and me much anxiety.

That night my wife and I had a long discussion over Anzic's possible surgery. We talked about the possibility of Anzic ever walking. We discussed what we could have done to avoid this, and what we could do now if we didn't choose the doctor's advice. We found ourselves caught in a corner without much choice.

The next day we called the hospital and asked to see the Shriners doctors again before they left the island. My wife and I hesitantly told them that we would allow our son to have the surgery.

We sensed a feeling of relief from the Shriners doctors, as well as those from our own hospital personnel, when we told them our decision. This gave us some comfort that perhaps we had made the right decision. I felt a sense of hope for Anzic, thinking he would be made whole again. He would finally have his legs fixed and be given a chance to walk and become like every kid. My hopes were sky high for him, and I prayed that he would have what we hoped he would have — a normal life.

Before my wife and Anzic left for Hawaii, I asked my wife to check with the doctors in Hawaii about why Anzic was still unable to talk, and why he still couldn't eat solid food.

I was sure I would get my answers when my wife returned with Anzic. This was in the year 2012.

At that time, one of my major job responsibilities was to coordinate Palau's participation in the 2012 Yeosu Expo in Korea. So, while my wife and Anzic left for the surgery in Hawaii, I took my three daughters, Talitha (Balie), Ja-el (O.B.) and Janel (Dilbi) and headed to Korea. I was the commissioner of a section for the Palau Pavilion in the Yeosu Expo in Korea, and I had to be in Yeosufor the Expo's closing. My wife and Anzic had gone to Hawaii, and we could talk through Skype, but this was expensive, since my wife had to buy an internet card to do it. In Yeosu, internet service was free, because we lived in the Expo village.

I felt for my wife and my son, but more for my son, because I'd brought my wife to Korea for the Expo's Palau National Day back in June. Both my wife and my youngest daughter enjoyed the Yeosu Expo festivities associated with the Palau National Day, which was observed on June 13, 2012. But my son Anzic never had the chance to even step on the airplane. Talking to him through Skype made me realize how much Anzic had missed out because of his disability. He had missed this most wonderful time in which children experience the ocean in a virtual as well as real world.

I was so sorry that Anzic had to miss out on this wonderful experience because he had to go to Hawaii for surgery. I strongly felt that he should have come with us on this trip. I felt that he belonged with his sisters and would have enjoyed this wonderful trip to Korea along with them. But his condition brought him to Hawaii instead.

This really didn't make the Korea trip go well, and I often Skyped with my wife to see how they both were doing in Hawaii. My mind was on Anzic and feeling sorry for him.

The surgery took place, requiring the doctors to break Anzic's legs right below the ball of the femur bone. They had to bend the bone so it could go into the socket, then bolted it there and braced the broken bone with stainless steel hardware, which was to remain there for a year before it could be removed.

After I returned to Palau, my wife sent me a picture of Anzic. I looked at it, and I cried. He was in a cast from his ankles to halfway up his belly. His legs were spread wide, and there was a bar that appeared to hold his legs apart. His movement was restricted so he couldn't walk, crawl, or even slide anywhere because of the cast. He also couldn't be loaded into a wheelchair to be pushed around. So, he basically slept everyday in this very uncomfortable position. He would have to be stuck like this for as long as the cast was on him. I could only imagine the discomfort and the frustration he must have felt.

When my wife told me that they had finally removed the cast, I cried again. But this time it was a cry of relief. I informed the church members and asked for their prayers and support. They were very encouraging and tried to comfort us with supporting words and Bible verses. I welcomed anything to help me get over Anzic's operation. I often wondered if we had made the right choice. I also often wondered, if Anzic were older, whether he would have chosen to have the surgery or not.

When people spoke to me about my son, I felt so helpless, and I became discouraged and very sad. My son's condition was on my mind all the time.

I sometimes spoke to God out loud: "How could You allow this to happen to Anzic? What did he do? Why does he have to suffer so much? If I am the sinner who caused all this, why won't you punish me, and allow him to have a normal life just like any other child?" Anzic had received such a harsh treatment, a punishment that perhaps was a result of a big sin. Sometimes I asked: Was it Anzic's fault? Did he sin? Or was it my sin? Did I sin that caused him to be like that?

I was sure there had to be an answer somewhere in the Bible.

I was hurting, knowing that Anzic lay there every day in such a disabled condition. I could hear David's cry in Psalm 6:2-9:

> *Be merciful to me, LORD, for I am faint.*
> *O LORD, heal me, for my bones are in agony.*
> *My soul is in anguish. How long O LORD, how long?*
> *Turn, O LORD, and deliver me; save me because of your unfailing love.*
> *I am worn out from groaning. All night long I flood my bed with weeping.*
> *My eyes grow weak with sorrow, they fail because of all my foes.*
> *Away from me, all you who do evil, for the LORD has heard my weeping.*
> *The LORD has heard my cry for mercy; the LORD accepts my prayer.*

David's prayer helped me to look at Anzic with a different perspective.

Despite the restrained condition Anzic was in, from the time he was small, he had a joyful spirit. He seemed to find joy in the little things he did, such as annoying his sisters, giving his daddy a hard time, teasing his caretaker, meeting people, talking in public, wheeling through the community, talking to Sumba (our neighbor's cat), and scaring Fluffy (our dog).

We would get really angry at him sometimes when he grabbed a container of baby powder that we'd left within his reach, and he emptied its contents on the floor. Or he crawled to the fridge and poured milk in our Parmesan cheese, or water into kimchi base, or ketchup into our drinking water. Sometimes he would get containers from the fridge and pour out their contents onto the floor, then mix it with his hands. Sometimes he would crack an egg or two in the mix.

This got on our nerves. When we found him making a mess and called his name in an angry voice, he would quickly try to make an even bigger mess before we could grab him and take him away from the situation. He would laugh his heart out, as if he'd just won a victory. When we got really angry, he would apologize with a simple "Sorry," followed by a kiss, a thrown kiss, or lots of laughter. As much as we wanted to spank him sometimes, we were stopped by his full enjoyment of the situation, so we would let him be.

He also enjoyed some intimate times. He would come and lean on us, seeking that loving touch. He would try to start a conversation, and he would enjoy quality time when we did things with him, such as playing cars, drawing, telling stories, or reading books. Sometimes he would also enjoy it when Dilbi, his sister, played the Samsung tablet and allowed him to watch and learn.

At times he would want to go places. If we told him we were busy and couldn't take him where he wanted to go, he wouldn't really complain. He had a look of understanding and acceptance of the fact that we couldn't take him at that time. When we felt guilty and promised to take him later, he would nod his head; sometimes he would say, "Okay," and he would smile, then turn back to whatever he was doing. But he does remember! So, when you walked by him, he would ask again.

When we were finally free and could take him out, he would laugh and sometimes shout with joy, and he'd happily accept our help to take him where he wanted to go. He never held a grudge like normal kids do; he wouldn't say, "Never mind, I asked you before, and you didn't want to do it." He simply accepted our offer of help whenever we were ready to offer it, and he did it with so much joy and excitement.

I wasn't so sure how Anzic would behave when he came home from Hawaii, and I didn't want him to lose this spirit of joy.

My children and I all missed him on his first trip to Hawaii for treatment. When my wife finally told us they were coming home, we were so excited and happy. We couldn't wait to go to the airport to see him. When he arrived and was pushed to greet us by an airport employee, my kids and I rushed to him. He seemed so happy to see us, and he talked a lot, bubbling out things we couldn't understand. While his language was hardly understood, it was obvious he was thrilled to see us and happy to be home.

After we arrived home, Anzic was very verbal and kept on talking. It was very unfortunate that we couldn't understand what he said. As I reflect on it now, I am touched that God heard my cry for mercy; He heard my plea for help, just as he had heard King David's plea. I was thinking, "Anzic had the surgery, and he now has a chance to use his legs and maybe even walk."

When I had the opportunity, I asked my wife if the doctors in Hawaii said anything about his condition. Did he really have cerebral palsy, as my daughter Balie had assessed? Or was it something that would change, and he would become normal? She told me that the doctors didn't tell her anything about his condition, but she also said she overheard them say that he does have a condition. What exactly was that condition? They never made this clear to her.

So, we continued to hope and pray and ask God for a miracle.

Anzic's Early Years

Recovery and enjoying life after surgery (2012)

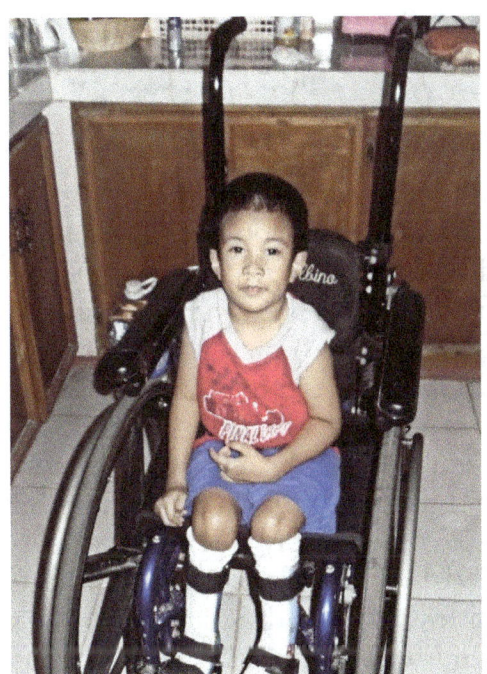

Anzic Alexander is recovering at the Shriners hospital in Hawaii and came home with a wheelchair bought by Shriners Hospital. Below is the family picture before the big surgery in Hawaii. (2012)

6

The Year after the First Hip Surgery

After returning home, we watched Anzic with great anticipation. Was he going to walk? Would he be able to stand on his legs? Would he be able to use crutches? There seemed to be so many potentials, but they were all without a clear answer. So, we continued to watch and hope. For Anzic, he took each day in stride. He entered first grade at Koror Elementary School as a special education student.

Attending school presented different challenges to be faced. There was a special bus for disabled children, and it came to pick him up. Anzic could simply ride in his wheelchair, which was provided by Shriners Hospital through donation. The bus would lower its hydraulic lift, and we would wheel him onto the lift platform. The hydraulic lift would take him to the level of the bus so he could easily ride inside. Once inside, they would secure his wheelchair so it wouldn't move while the bus was moving, and then he would be ready to go. Regina, our Filipina helper, rode the bus with him because the program required someone to accompany him to school. While Anzic was at school, Regina also helped with his personal needs and with his food.

Anzic was just happy to ride the bus and be in school. There were other children who would ride with him, and he seemed to enjoy their company. However, we started to notice a few things that were becoming very clear to us. Anzic didn't like any door slammed. Hearing that loud noise would make him get really angry. He also didn't appreciate people who coughed, sneezed, or cleared their throats; he would really get bothered by that. We also noticed that he didn't like whistles or any sort of hissing sound.

We also noticed that he had his favorites. He liked Mr. Bean and SpongeBob. He also liked music shows and could easily pick up and carry a tune. In fact, we were told that his favorite song during church services in Hawaii was "How Great Thou Art," and that he could sing along with everyone on that and other songs.

We saw that our son was growing and was starting to show the characteristics of young children that make them so dear. It made him all the more precious to us.

My wife and I were very grateful for the help we got from Regina, our Filipina helper. She was very helpful with the work around the house, but most importantly in helping Anzic. She was like a mother to him and would get up early and prepare his food, shower him in the morning, dress him for school, and take him to school. She would defend him at school like her own son and would always go to his assistance. Sometimes this irritated the teachers, and they would call us and complain that Regina went to his rescue even when the teachers raised their voices to him because he refused instruction. She would scold the teachers, telling them they had to teach Anzic while he was in a learning mood and open to instruction; otherwise, they were wasting his time, and their instruction would irritate him.

Throughout his first year at school, Anzic was always on time and enjoyed most of his days there. His teachers noticed that he wasn't afraid to try things, except when it came to food. Also, he would go right up to the principal and ask to use the bullhorn, which the principal used to make announcements during school assemblies. Once given the bullhorn, he would sing and make noise into it to the amusement of the rest of the students. Other students, young and old, liked him for his boldness, his wheelchair, and his clear expression of how he feels without any reservation. When he wanted to be in the crowd, he would wheel his wheelchair right into their midst; when he didn't want to be bothered, he would tell those around him to go away.

He did this with students and teachers alike.

When Christmas came around, Anzic was so excited and happy. We took him around to see the Christmas lights and cruised around town to look at the different decorations. He could sense that something exciting was coming up, and he was happy to be part of whatever was going to happen. Finally, the school program came. The first-grade part was simply to sing. Anzic sat in his wheelchair and cheered while his classmates sang. He seemed to enjoy their singing as a listener and didn't realize he was a performer along with his classmates. But he had so much fun, and we were excited to see him that way.

His healing progress seemed slow. Several times we took him to Dr. Bhotoo, a local orthopedic specialist, for follow-up visits. The hardware (we weren't sure if they were stainless or plastic) was still embedded in his body, holding the bones together. Dr. Bhotoo started to explain to us that Anzic's condition wasn't going to improve. This was the first doctor who told us that our son would never walk. Dr. Bhotoo told us that Anzic also had a condition called osteoporosis, in which the body doesn't process the nutrition needed for the bones, causing those bones to lose density and become fragile. This condition stunts bone growth and causes them to become thin and weak.

This was a big blow to us, since we had all hoped that the surgery in Hawaii would help Anzic to be able to walk. But Dr. Bhotoo explained that the surgery was to take away the constant pain caused by the bones being separated from the socket joint of the hipbone, not to enable him to walk. He told us to be careful with him, since his bones are very delicate. So, for the next year, we babied Anzic. We were very careful with his activities and where he went. If he appeared not to like something, we would go to his rescue and try to make him as comfortable as possible. After about a year, he returned to Hawaii to remove the hardware.

This time we were starting to understand his situation,

and so we weren't as anxious as we were the first time. We felt we'd become familiar with the process and knew what was going to happen. Anzic and my wife left for Hawaii. All three of the older girls were at home, with Balie attending Palau Community College, Ja-el attending Bethania High School, and our youngest daughter, Dilbi, attending Koror Elementary School.

When Anzic went to the second surgery, the doctors were surprised to see that the point where they joined the broken bone of the left leg wasn't healing. In fact, it had separated, with space in between. To fix that problem, they needed to extend the lower bone so it could be attached to the upper bone. The doctors agreed to graft the bones, meaning they would insert new bone between the two bones that were separated and hope it would be adopted and become part of the bone. It was hoped that the inserted foreign bone would connect the two femur bones that were broken, so they could heal and become one.

Anzic stayed in Hawaii for a while because the doctors wanted to wait for the new bone to be attached to the old bones before releasing him to come home. The length of stay this time was about three months.

A few months after that first surgery, Anzic either fell or slipped and reinjured his left hipbone. This caused a loosening in the point where the doctors joined the bone. It also fractured the lower part of the femur bone close to the knee joint. We were aware of the fracture because we took Anzic to the hospital when it happened. However, we were told by Dr. Bhotoo that since the bones weren't separated, it was best not to apply a cast. We just had to be careful with his movements, and thus allow the fracture to heal. So, it didn't appear to be a big issue, but it did lengthen his time in Hawaii before he returned home.

In 2013, we had to make a return trip to Hawaii to adjust the brace on Anzic's hip. The bones got separated and did not heal properly.

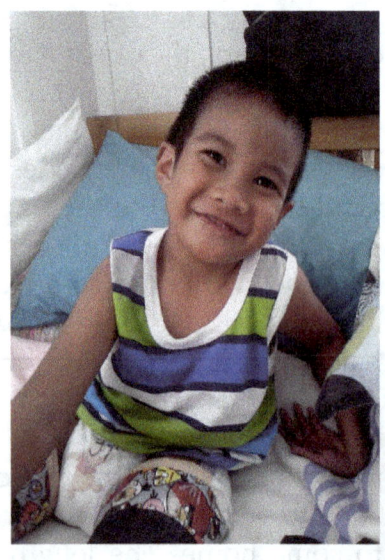

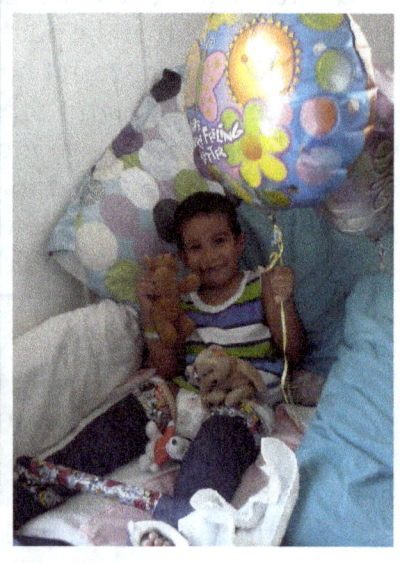

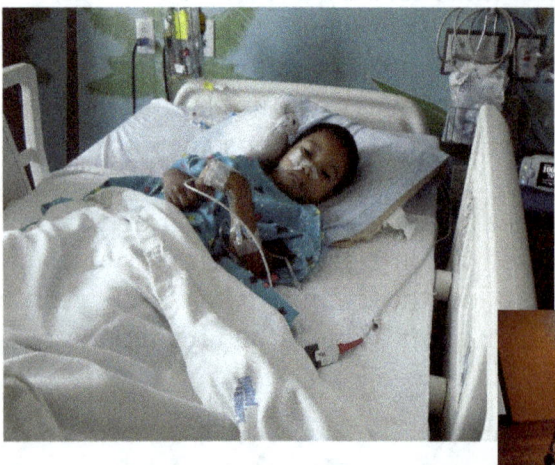

The second trip resulted in more work on the left hip joint.

The Year after the First Hip Surgery

In 2013, before the surgery, the doctors removed Anzic's front teeth as they were concerned about any infection. He still like to brush his teeth and smile as well. He also learned to hang on to the bar separating his legs for support and would sit up straight. He didn't and still doesn't really like to just lay around or sleep. He is very active and prefers moving around.

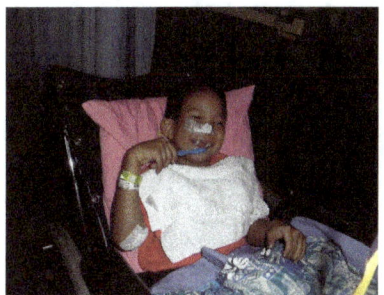
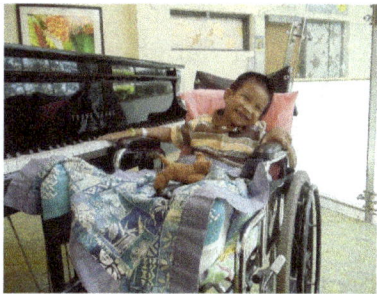
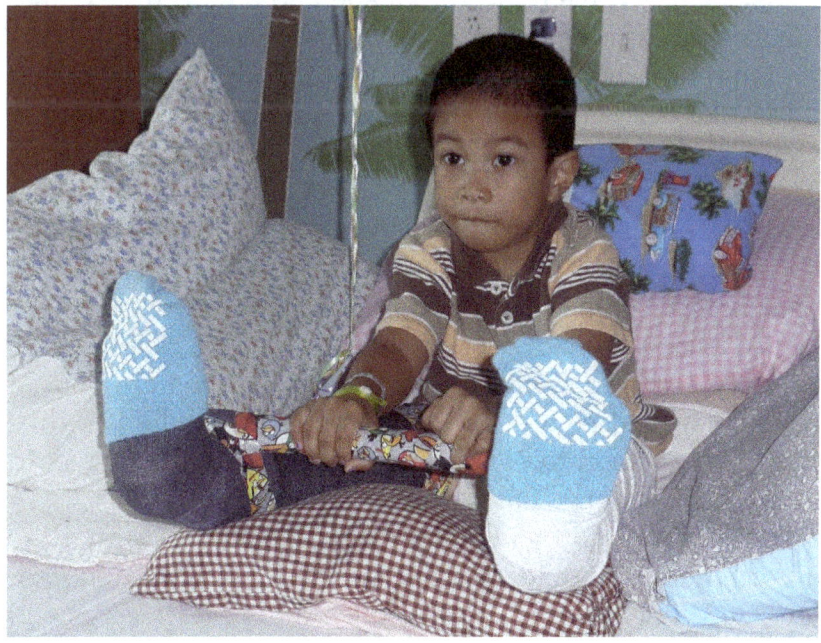

7

Anzic's Sister Dilbi

We never forgot the sibling who was closest in age to Anzic. Our daughter Dilbi, whose real name is Janel, was a grade higher than Anzic, and two years older. She was born prematurely at six months and spent the first three months of her life in an incubator. She was so tiny and needed to be fed by tubes and IVs. We weren't even sure if she would live. After she was three months old, she was released from the hospital, but she was still so small and red that people were afraid to touch her.

As she grew, we noticed that she had a hard time crawling. Instead, she just tried to get up and stand on her feet. As soon as she was able to stand, she would hang on to something like her bed or the TV stand, and she would slowly walk around it. It wasn't long before she was walking on her own. She accomplished this soon after her first birthday. Through sheer determination, she simply skipped crawling and went straight from lying down to walking. She's an amazing girl with the most positive spirit I know.

She learned to run quickly and had a lot of energy. She was even able to climb out of the Chinese bed we bought her that was three feet off the ground. She could also dive into it. But I soon took the bed out for fear that she would break her neck or her arm or something.

We also noticed that Dilbi didn't quite walk as straight as a normal child would, and she seemed to be dragging her left leg. When she ran, she was unable to bend her legs and ran straight-legged. When we brought her to the doctor at Belau National Hospital, we were told that this was a result of the premature birth. We were also informed that there would be more issues as she grew older. But my mother, bless her heart, assured us that this isn't always the case. Her cousin Sadako, who became her closest companion, was born prematurely just like our daughter. My mother kept saying, "If you see Sadako now, you would never know she was a premature baby."

When Dilbi started school, she had to repeat first grade. I never doubted that God had a plan, but it was harder for us, as parents, then it was for Dilbi. I figured it had to do with her premature birth, but I was also frustrated with the school system. Her progress reports showed great progress, but when she received her report cards, she had failed. The teacher said this was due to her not passing the quarterly assessment tests. But she did quite well her second year in school.

As Dilbi grew, she showed other problems and also was showing signs of cerebral palsy. She was placed on the high-risk list and would visit the children's doctors every three months. But Dilbi didn't want to be left behind, and her goal was to enjoy everything. When we asked her, "Why do we go to school?" her immediate response with glee would be, "To play!" Studying as the main goal for going to school was never considered; it was only a part of the program. Finally, in fourth grade, she started to show signs of seriousness. She didn't want to miss her homework; she didn't want to get an F; she wanted to receive praise from her teacher, and she wanted to pass her grades. Still, she had no sense of competition. She would be fine with other children doing better than she did. In fact, she praised other kids, saying, "That girl, she's very smart." I think that at this point she didn't want to be retained again, so she began working a little harder on her studies. But when reminded that school is for studying, she always added, "and play also."

Dilbi and Anzic have gotten along really well, although Dilbi would be happy with anyone as long as they didn't bully her or take advantage of her. Dilbi's handicap, if any, would be that she sees life as it is. She doesn't understand lies and doesn't quite understand when we try to play tricks on others. So, anything that appears a bit out of the ordinary would be roll-on-the-floor funny to her. Sometimes she would get a big kick out of her own thoughts and would go into a laughing frenzy, much to the amusement of everyone around her.

Anzic would always be amused by Dilbi when she started laughing. He laughed at first and then tried to figure out what was funny. When he didn't get it, he would get annoyed by the laughter and would start to argue with her. Because he liked to pick on people, he often crawled next to Dilbi when she was occupied with the TV, and he would scratch her slightly. She wouldn't pay attention to him. He would continue at this until she got annoyed and would scream. This would get him on a laughing frenzy, as he would try to crawl as if escaping. He also liked to grab a crayon or a marker and run it across Dilbi's drawings. He'd laugh, even though she would get irritated. To him, it was a game, and he looked for every chance to laugh and have fun. We really enjoyed being around this funny pair.

While in Hawaii for the third surgery, Anzic kept asking for Dilbi. I felt that he missed children his age because he was always around his parents and our two older daughters, Balie and O.B. When we mentioned Dilbi's name, he would cry. So, my wife and I decided we were going to bring Dilbi to Hawaii for Christmas so he could see her.

With the help of our relative who worked for the airlines, this was made possible. When we arrived in Hawaii, we dropped our bags at the apartment shared by our daughters Balie and O.B., and we all headed to Shriners Hospital. My daughters, sister-in-law, and even Dilbi couldn't wait to see Anzic's reaction when he finally saw Dilbi.

Anzic and my wife were in their room. So, we put him in his wheelchair and took him to the "open space" area where his sisters were waiting. He was happy to see them all but especially ecstatic that Dilbi was there. He wheeled his chair around as fast as he could and kept saying, "Dilbi, Dilbi, Dilbi." It was like he was trying to show her something or express something to her. It was very apparent that his joy was so full at that moment.

Like any siblings, they would have their fights, quarrels, and annoying moments. But they would also have their fun times, good times, sharing, and loving moments. Dilbi would always be concerned if anything happened to Anzic or if there was something out of the ordinary for him. She would want to know if he was okay.

Janel "Delbochel" Alexander, Anzic's older sister

Dilbi has been Anzic's companion most of the time. When he was in Hawaii for the third surgery, he kept asking for her. When she finally arrived in Hawaii, he was very happy to be with her. Dilbi has been blessed as she has traveled to many parts of the world, but Anzic has not had that opportunity. But God's blessings are overflowing regardless.

The photo to the left won a prize from the Telecommunication company. Anzic with a phone, Janel with the TV & Ja-el on the internet.

Janel has been to Shanghai, China for the 2010 World Expo as well as the 2012 World Expo in Yeosu Korea.

Janel enjoys time with her sisters and really likes swimming.

8

Anzic's Favorite Activities

We have been amazed by Anzic's ability to take full joy in situations, and this has enabled us to see God's work in his life. Even though our son showed signs of frustration because of not being able to do what he wanted to do, he also accepted what we could do for him. Some of his favorite activities that gave evidence of this included riding in a car around town. This was probably his favorite activity of all. He loved the feeling of the ride and the chance to explore and look around. He knew the roads and where they led, and he asked to go to certain places. If we chose to go in a different direction, he wouldn't complain, but simply accepted our choice.

Christmas time was his favorite time to ride. He loved the decorations and asked for a ride almost every evening. His excitement often compelled us to take him for those rides, and our excitement came from watching him enjoy every moment of them. He just simply enjoyed the cruise and the scenery. He would have stayed out all day doing so if it were possible, just for the joy it brings. When the time came to return home, he'd let us know he didn't want to go home, but he accepted this also and would be content.

His second favorite activity was to be put in his wheelchair and walked around the neighborhood. He enjoyed seeing people and talking to them. When we were unable to take him out when he wanted to go, we could tell him, "Later," and he would sit and quietly watch TV or play with his small cars without making a big fuss—no tantrums or complaints. He, like our other children, was always obedient to what we asked, a quality that I've prayed will transfer to their relationship with the Lord.

I've learned much from Anzic about how our relationship with God should be. He has modeled how we are to happily accept what is offered us by God, and not complain about what we don't have. This ability is a godly characteristic and brings us much closer to Him.

When I read or hear the stories of the heroes in the Bible, I'm amazed at how they accepted what God gave them. These are people who made history, who fathered our faith, and who gave us prime examples to follow—people like Abraham, Isaac, Jacob, Joseph, Moses, Gideon, Samuel, David, and the list goes on.

One particular story that I can relate to while living each day with Anzic is the story in 1 Samuel 16 about the prophet Samuel visiting Jesse, the father of David. Samuel offered a sacrifice and then chose David, as directed by the Lord, to be anointed as the next king of Israel. David was still a boy when he was anointed king, and at that time, Saul still held the position of being Israel's king. Yet, right after David was anointed, he went back to watching his father's flock. He never asked his father to find another shepherd to watch the flock because it was no longer a suitable job for him as the future king of Israel. At the end of the same chapter, we read that God put David under King Saul's service.

How many of us, knowing that we've been appointed by God for a certain position, would willingly serve the person who currently sits there?

There are kingdoms, governments, and nations that go into turmoil because even before the sitting president or prime minister is removed, someone starts proclaiming that he deserves to be in that position. Many allegations come out, much opposition arises, and sometimes demonstrations, fighting, and looting breaks loose. There are offices in traditional governments, democratic governments, and all kinds of governments that fall into disarray when people in lower positions create problems in the office because they want the higher position. To get there, they bring allegations and false accusations, and they create turmoil in the office so they can get rid of the person at the helm, and then they can move in and take over.

Who are the real victims of such problems? It's the people who depend on the government and on the country's economy to survive. The services are disrupted, and the economy turns against the people who are supposed to benefit from it.

David did no such thing. He didn't hold anything against King Saul, nor did he try to get Saul removed so he could take over.

When the Spirit of God left King Saul, an evil spirit tormented him. This was right after David had been anointed king. David could have easily tried to convince Saul that this torment by an evil spirit was a sign that Saul should resign, and then David could become king. But David did no such thing.

When David entered Saul's service, Saul liked him (1 Samuel 16:21). It's obvious David didn't try to compete with Saul for the throne. He took his service seriously and humbled himself. Even David's father, old Jesse, who might have imagined wealth and power as the father of a king, humbled himself and sent gifts to King Saul (1 Samuel 16:20). Even before David went to serve Saul, Saul's servant said this about David: "He is a brave man and a warrior. He speaks well and is a fine-looking man. And the Lord is with him."

At this point, David, although he has been anointed king of Israel, took the role of a servant. He did a very good job of serving Saul because Saul liked him. Saul even sent word to Jesse, saying, "Allow David to remain in my service, for I am pleased with him" (1 Samuel 16:22).

While Anzic will never be like David in physical appearance, and perhaps even in spirit and faith, he reflects the same spirit of acceptance as David. Whatever circumstances we put Anzic in, he looks for the fun part of it and is willing to accept what we offer. He doesn't complain much; he airs his opposition only when we ask him to do something we know he doesn't like.

Even as a youth, David must have shown signs of a fine warrior's appearance. It would seem that he was increasingly tall, handsome, and well-built. Anzic is short, crippled, and unable to walk. I'm not sure about the good-looking part, although many say he is. But one thing is for sure: Anzic is willing to be what we ask him to be and enjoys it. He offers the brightest smile if given the slightest bit of attention.

Anzic will never in his lifetime play soccer or basketball or volleyball. He'll never walk in a walkathon for the school. He'll never chase other children in their games. He'll never go swimming or fishing or do any water sports. We feel somehow that he's deprived of some of the best things in life. I know when he watches kids play in the area, he longs to play, and perhaps even to run, with them. Yet he does what he can, raising his hands in the air and screaming like them, and exhibiting the same joy and happiness that other children do.

My wife and I really struggled when Dr. Bhotoo told us that Anzic would never walk. My heart sank to the bottom of the sea. Many nights after that, I cried in bed, knowing that Anzic would never experience life as I have. But he does enjoy to the fullest the life he has been given. He accepts whatever comes his way, small or big, and enjoys it as much as he can. He has no attitude of entitlement, as many do. It breaks my heart to watch him in his limitations, but he seems much better than I am. He most certainly is full of spirit.

Around the house, Anzic often lays in front of the television and plays with his cars. Sometimes he would engage in three activities at a time and would laugh and scream with joy as he is absorbed in his activities. He would often line up his toy cars and play with them; he would also turn on our old laptop and watch a movie on it while playing with his toy cars; he would also grab my Samsung tablet and play a game on it while watching television and playing with his cars. I noticed that he likes to play Minecraft on the Samsung tablet as his older sister Janel plays it often. While his older sister Janel enjoys building and constructing structures, Anzic enjoys destroying them with fire.

Janel gets irritated by Anzic's behavior because she likes new creations and enjoys building and constructing structures. She can construct a whole city with walls, yards, tall buildings, small buildings, and so forth. Whenever she leaves the tablet around, Anzic would grab it and destroy all with fire. When Janel returns to the tablet, she would notice what he has done, and she would scream at him, but he seems to get a real kick out of what he has done and laughs. Of course, this irritates his older sister even more. Perhaps it is negative behavior, but he seems to enjoy the attention he gets from her even though it may be negative. Of course, at times he would sit there and watch her play without disturbing her. It is as if he just likes being next to her and being a part of her activity.

Anzic's favorite show is Sponge Bob. He knows its schedule by memory and would ask for the TV to be turned there when it is time. Some parts of the show scare him, and he would hide his face and block his ears during certain portions of the show. We have tried to find out which parts of the Sponge Bob shows scare him. It is hard to tell because sometimes it is certain noises that scare him, sometimes it is a character he doesn't like, sometimes he does it because of external noises that have nothing to do with the show. So, to this day, we are still not sure what scares him, and Sponge Bob is still his favorite show. When we turn on the TV, he will look at the time or outside (sun's direction) to determine the time of day. He would then direct us to his favorite show, and if it is not on, he would not mind other

Anzic's Favorite Activities

channels except ESPN, Dad's favorite channel.

He would be fine with foreign programs like the Korean channel, KBS, which is Mom's favorite channel or the news. But he will not even allow ESPN to be on while he is in the living room. For some reason, he doesn't like NHK, the Japanese channel. He also really enjoys the music programs, especially those on TBN, the Christian network, or Hope, the other Christian network. He also enjoys the music shows on KBS and seems to sing along with the program at times. But he doesn't accept the Japanese music as much as he does the other music. Even on the radio, he would listen to local music, English, even Korean, but he will block his ears when Japanese songs are played.

He is very attentive to people coming in and out of the house. When he is engaged in his many activities, he will quickly look up when I appear in the living room. He will often ask me to take him. He would first ask "Kamor" which means 'where are you going?' His pronunciation is a little blurred, but it is clear enough for anyone to know that he is asking about where the person would be going. He would follow by saying "Ma Mei." This is a combination of some words that he had managed to put together to express himself. 'Ma' means 'and' which in reference to people would mean 'and me.' It is sort like the English expression of 'go away' which means 'you go away,' but you don't say the 'you.' 'Ma' in reference to people means 'and me too,' but you don't need to say the 'too.' 'Mei' means 'come.' In context to this the phrase of 'me too' it would translate to 'take me with you.'

So, whenever I grab my hat, my small bag, put on a new shirt, or simply grab my keys, he would look at me with those longing eyes and say 'Ma Mei' meaning take me with you. I often tell him that I have to do some errand but will come back and take him when it is time to play or to stroll around. He would nod his head in acknowledgment and would turn back to his activities. One thing I have learned to appreciate from my children is that they never cry or throw a tantrum whenever they want to tag along on a trip. Anzic seems to be the same. He would ask to go with me or his mom, but when we say no, with an explanation, he seems to accept it and not cry about it. As a reward, whenever I become free on those days that he asks, I would take him on a ride. If the weather was good, we would stop by the church, and I would put him on his wheelchair and walk him around the church grounds, the Emmaus-Bethania campus and even in the baseball field. When he gets tired, he would ask me to take him inside the church and then ask me to sit so he can wheel himself around the church. I would hear him sing 'How Great Thou Art' one of his favorite songs.

We have come to understand that even with all his activities, he longs to go out and see outside and ride around town. I often take him out, and we simply stroll down to the old Japanese airport ramp on the other side of the island and back to the new airport where he enjoys looking at airplanes even when they are just sitting there. When we go through the middle part of town in downtown Koror, where there are big crowds of people, he would roll his window down and say 'Hi' to everyone that walks by. Cars cannot go fast in this part of town, so people would hear him and would say 'Hi' back. He seems to really enjoy that as though he had made new friends.

Going past the Japan-Palau Friendship Bridge, which connects the Commercial Center of Koror with the Big Island of Babeldaob where the airport is, he would start singing a song about Airai state, the first state of Babeldaob we come to when we cross the bridge. He first heard the song on TV, and when the song played, it showed the picture of the Bridge. The song is 'Airai a Koted' meaning 'Airai is our origin.' He has remembered the song and attached it to the Bridge that whenever we come to the bridge, he would sing it. One thing for sure, his memory is quite good because the song came out on TV about three years ago. He still remem-

Anzic's Favorite Activities

bers it to this day.

When we go to the airport, he would ask that we sit there and watch the airplanes. Sometimes, when we are lucky, a small airplane would come or would get ready to leave. He would be glued to that airplane as though he is studying it. He would utter words that I cannot understand, but he appears to be saying some things about the airplane. When the airplane takes off, he would scream with joy as though he was on it.

When I look at him when he is very happy, a part of me is wishful that he would not grow up. At times, I wish he would stay the same and not grow an inch or even mature a little. Although he is now 11 years old, he is like a baby still learning about things and how to talk. He knows he is fully dependent on us. At times, he tries to be assertive and imposes his wants on us, but always, he would submit and obey what we say, and he would do it with contentment. It is as if he accepts what we offer him.

Anzic really enjoys going to church. He loves singing along with the people when they sing, and he has memorized a number of church songs to which he can sing along. When the congregation begins to sing a song that he knows, and there are quite a few, he will sing with the crowd, and he would sing loudly. He also enjoys watching our church choir when they sing. That's probably the only time he would sit quietly and watch them sing. Other than that, he would always be singing or asking to leave or wanting to talk. He still hates it when people clear their throats or cough. So, when the little children in Sunday School come for their program, he would ask to leave. He knows many of them just cough without covering their mouths, and he gets irritated. He also would ask to leave whenever there are others in the congregation who does that. When we go by ourselves, he seems to enjoy it because there is no one to irritate him. He would wheel himself around and take in the joy of being in the church, although we are all alone. He would sing, hum, clap, scream and let himself go as though he truly belongs there. It makes me happy to know that he feels comfortable and at peace in the church sanctuary.

I would look at him, and those haunting thoughts would come back to me while we are inside the church. What is Anzic's purpose? Will he fulfill it? How would he glorify God in his state? I recall Matthew 15:30 where it says, 'Great crowds came to Him, bringing the lame, the blind, the mute, and many others and laid them at His feet; and He healed them.' I would look up at the altar and wonder if our presence there qualifies as bringing Anzic to Jesus' feet and laying him there. If I called on Jesus to heal Anzic right there, would he do it? In the New Testament, especially in the Gospels, many who went to Jesus sought him for help especially healing. They sought healing for themselves, their children, their friends, or their servants. And Jesus was merciful and gracious and healed them one by one. Would he do that for Anzic? Would his purpose be to testify of God's healing, or was it something else his life was to testify to?

In Mark 2:1-12, Mark relays the story of the four men who brought a paralytic to Jesus when he was in Capernaum. The house was so crowded that they went up on the roof and broke the roof open to lower the man to Jesus. Jesus, seeing their faith, forgave the sins of the paralytic and healed him so he walked home with his bed.

The Gospel of John chapter 5 (John 5:1-15) tells an additional story. Near the Pool of Bethesda, an invalid sat for thirty-eight years, not able to bring himself to the pool for healing when it is stirred by an angel. He told Jesus that whenever he tries to get in, someone goes in before him. Jesus felt compassion for him and healed him; so, he got up and took his mat and walked. Remembering these stories bring many questions to my mind. Did I have enough faith to heal Anzic? Was the boy from Victory Chapel correct in saying that if I possessed faith, Anzic would be healed?

Have I failed as a man of God and as a father to heal Anzic? Was healing Anzic God's purpose and will, or was it just my desire?

Anzic is curious just like any kid and enjoys many things all kids enjoy.

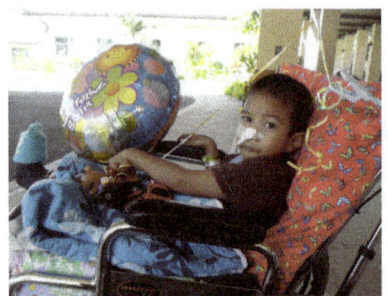

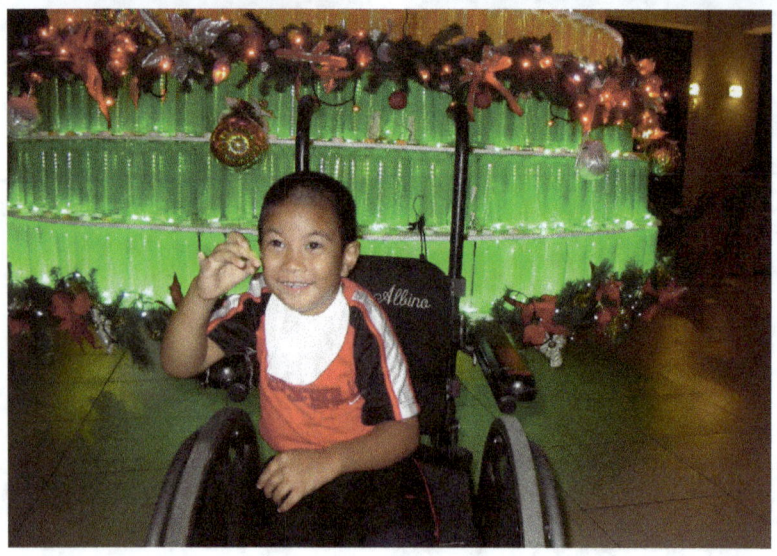

Like every kid, Anzic enjoys toys, especially his cars. He also enjoys things that fly; even a balloon would do. But most of all, he enjoys people, and every person he meets he finds a liking to. He enjoys school because there are many children there, and there are many activities. He also enjoys church and being around people who sing. He likes good singers and knows when someone cannot sing worth a tune. Above is a Christmas celebration where he really liked the lights and the ornaments, just as he did in Hawaii.

Anzic's Favorite Activities

Anzic enjoying school sports day, leisure by the pool with mom, Halloween costume in 2015, Christmas 2015 and a visit from family on December 24, 2015 after the cyst surgery.

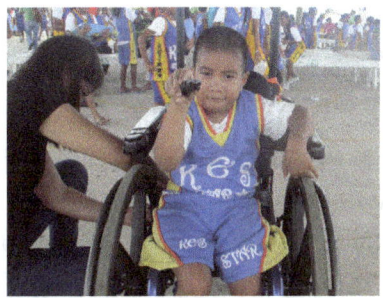
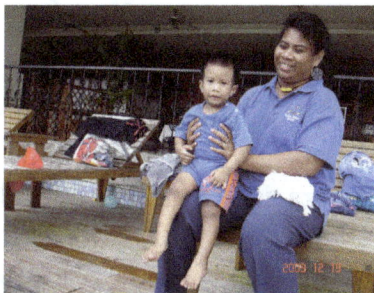
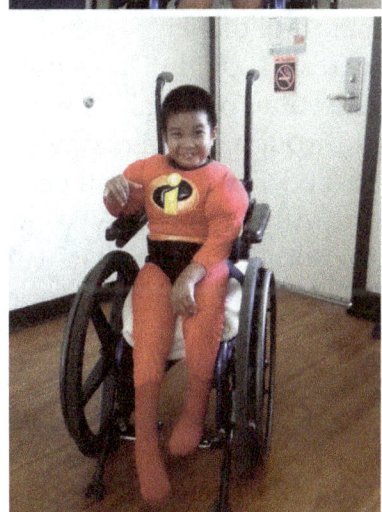
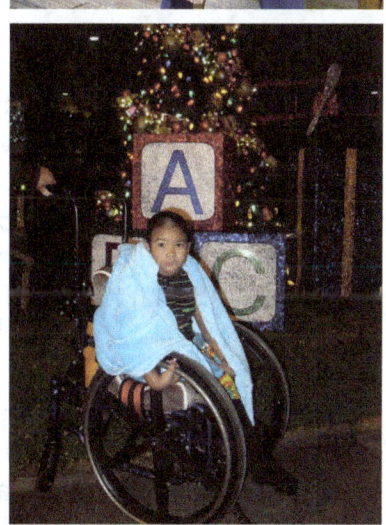
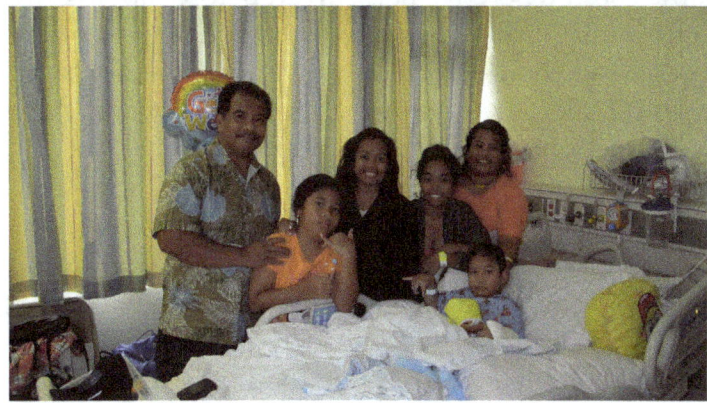

9

Back to the Drawing Board

After submitting our Med-QUEST application, my wife and I discussed many things, including the roles of Shriners Hospital, the social workers, Kapi'olani Medical Center, and the Palau medical coordinator. We discussed a number of options for funding and possible ways to get Anzic's much-needed operation at Kapi'olani.

With each discussion, we prayed and sought God's guidance. We decided to meet with the Palau medical coordinator to see if they could see a way through all the confusion. My wife called Ms. Allyn and asked if we could meet to discuss Anzic's medical treatment. Allyn agreed. When we arrived for our meeting with her, other people that were present. We felt that maybe this wasn't the right time for us to express our concerns; perhaps we should handle these things ourselves, and we shouldn't bother the medical coordinator. After all, we were there at the request of Shriners Hospital, and not the Palau medical coordinator's office.

But Ms. Allyn came and said we could meet. We met in the same room where we had stayed before moving to Shriners Hospital. Once away from everybody else, I offered to pray before we had our talk. I prayed a rather short prayer that was emotional, not only for me but everyone. After we prayed, Mr. Uchel Naito came and joined us.

To begin, I explained that we understood how God had a hand in all of this, but we just weren't quite sure where it was leading. We sought understanding by finding out all the possible options to pave the way for the cyst surgery and the hip surgery, which needed to be done in that order. I also explained that I understood they were very busy,

Back to the Drawing Board

but we wanted to know if they had considered Anzic's case and if they clearly understood what had transpired. They acknowledged that they knew and understood.

Ms. Allyn explained that it was a sign of God's people and of the members of his family that the tone and direction of our meeting was not argumentative or complaining. She assured us that they, too, relied on God, not only for our case, but for all the cases they handled as the coordinating office. She explained that relying on God ensures a greater chance of success, as opposed to relying on their own abilities, knowledge, and experience in the work; they would always have to trust God for guidance in all that they do. So, they were pleased to hear that this is what we sought above all. We wanted to know God's purpose and will for this situation, and where He was leading us.

We looked at several options. One option was just to wait, since an application had been submitted to Med-QUEST. It was possible that they would agree to fund Anzic's surgery at Kapi'olani.

There were two other options as well. One was to return to Palau and request that the Palau Referral Office make a special appeal to Tripler Army Medical Center to consider extending their services to Anzic for the cyst surgery. Tripler also offers free services under the special agreement with Palau through the Compact of Free Association. The second option was to appeal for funding assistance from Palau's Health Care Fund (HCF), of which my wife and I were contributors and beneficiaries. Both options would require either my wife or me to return to Palau to make our plea.

After this meeting with Ms. Allyn, my wife and I returned to the Shriners Hospital Family Center and discussed which option was best to take. We were both hesitant about following through on the options that would require a return trip to Palau. We felt more comfortable dealing with this situation together and being available to help Anzic through this time.

It took us a couple of days to really think through these options. We understood that if Med-QUEST turned us down (which was likely), then Anzic wouldn't have the surgery unless one of the other options we had discussed with Ms. Allyn was approved. Reluctantly, we agreed that I would return to Palau to appeal to HCF and the Palau Referral Office.

I prepared myself, got my ticket, and returned to Palau. I immediately went to see the HCF administrator stationed at Palau's Social Security office. He told me that HCF is used only for referral to treatment in the Philippines and the Republic of China (Taiwan), and wasn't meant to be used in Hawaii at Tripler or Shriners. This made me angry. I understood the reasons, but in my view, the main purpose of HCF was to help Palauan citizens fund the medical services they so desperately needed. I felt that Anzic's case merited consideration since he was already in Hawaii. It was most certainly not recommended that he fly to Palau and then travel to the Philippines or Taiwan for this medical treatment.

I was advised to meet with the Palau Referral Office and with the Medical Savings Account (MSA) officials to see if they could perhaps fund this case. Meanwhile, I kept contact with my wife in Hawaii. She told me that our social worker at Shriners Hospital had advised her that if Med-QUEST didn't approve our request, she would bring our case back to the Shriners administration and make a push for them to fund it. She assured my wife that she need not worry. My wife then advised me not to pursue our request with MSA and the Palau Referral Office. She was concerned that the hospitals or Med-QUEST might withdraw their support if they found out that MSA, Palau Referral Office, or the HCF were seeking information about our case. And if Palau refused to fund the emergency hospitalization, we might be held liable for the costs incurred so far. Also, our social worker at Shriners said that even if MSA or the Palau HCF were to agree to pay, it probably wouldn't be full coverage.

So, I didn't go to the Palau Referral Office, and I didn't contact the MSA office. Instead, I went to prayer, with the understanding that if Med-QUEST turned down our request, and if Shriners Hospital made a final decision that they wouldn't fund the surgery, only then would I proceed to see MSA and the Palau Referral Office. I also shared my concerns in our Sunday evening service at church. I told the members that my entire family really needed prayer, as we were all affected by this whole series of events.

A couple of days later, my wife told me that Med-QUEST had approved our request and would fund all the treatment, including medicine for Anzic. We were so humbled to know that God had intervened on our behalf. We were ecstatic and joyous, while understanding that it was God who made this possible. We were so blessed! I nearly cried when my wife told me the news, and I realized that God knew and had already planned for this, while my wife, Ms. Allyn, Mr. Naito, and I were all scrambling for some sort of explanation and direction to take.

While all this was happening, Anzic was simply enjoying being in Hawaii. He wasn't a bit concerned about anything.

The psalmist writes, "I lift up my eyes toward the mountains. Where will my help come from? My help comes from the LORD, the Maker of heaven and the earth" (Psalm 121:1-2). Most assuredly, when we are lost and don't know where to turn, our God is only a step away, and He is ready to help and minister to our needs.

In 2 Corinthians 12:7-10, Paul tells us of his appeal to God regarding his weakness, when he couldn't see the end of the tunnel in his misery. He called it a "thorn in the flesh," "a messenger of Satan," and "a tormentor." Anzic's situation reflected my weakness before the Lord. I realized that I had as much of a handicap as Anzic had, and in the same way as Paul had. I would constantly panic, even though Paul's words are very reassuring, comforting, and guiding when we pay close attention to them.

Three times Paul had pleaded with the Lord to take away his "thorn in the flesh." But the Lord responded by telling Paul, "My grace is sufficient for you, for My power is made perfect in weakness." I realized that whenever I had a problem, I tried to solve the problem. I'm a problem-solver, and most everybody is. Whenever something feels like it needs fixing, we go into motion to try and get it fixed. Sometimes we even do it for things that don't need fixing.

We honestly don't want to have weaknesses, and we have a hard time admitting when we do. But when we see a weakness in our lives, we jump to try and fix it, mostly in our own physical strength and wisdom. We must accept the fact that our strength and wisdom are weak and faulty. We make mistakes, and we focus on the wrong causes.

Anzic clearly shows my wife and I how weak, helpless, and faulty our strength and abilities are, and how often we make mistakes and end up with the wrong results.

The Kapi'olani Medical Center was happy to hear the news about the Med-QUEST funding. They were assured payment for the time we'd spent there, and now also payment for the much needed surgery. They were as thrilled by the news as we were. They scheduled the surgery to take place on December 22, 2015. This allowed me to return to Hawaii with Dilbi over the Christmas break, and for us to be together as a family during the holidays.

On December 22, my wife and I brought Anzic to the hospital at 5:00 a.m. They prepped him for the surgery, and we were told the surgery would start at 7:30 and would finish in four hours. We headed to the counseling room to wait. The nurses brought a white suit like those worn by astronauts and said one of us could go into the surgery room to see it before the operation but couldn't stay inside once the surgery began.

My wife decided it would be me, since she couldn't wear that suit. So, I put on the suit, which covered me from head to toe. Dr. Sutherland came and took me in and showed me the robot that was going to operate on Anzic. He also showed me his station as the main surgeon. It looked like an arcade game with a big screen, and the robot was hanging over Anzic. The other doctors would assist by inserting the tentacles of the robot into Anzic, and Dr. Sutherland would do the rest. He would guide the robot tentacles inside Anzic's body around the bladder to the scar-tissue-like cyst, and he would slowly cut it out. Afterward, he would tie the tubes together, and if there were anything else that needed to be sown, he would do it with the robot. The incisions were to be very small, just big enough for the tentacles, which were about the size of a finger.

Before surgery began, I came out, and we decided to go back to the Shriners Hospital Family Center to eat and do some chores while we waited. At about 11:00 a.m., almost four hours into the surgery, we decided to return to the hospital. However, when we returned, the status on the screen indicated that Anzic's surgery was still in progress. We waited patiently for another hour or so. A nurse came and assured us that the doctor should be coming out soon to advise us about Anzic's status. We waited until about one o'clock or shortly after.

It was nearly six hours into the surgery when the nurse told us to move to the counseling room. We were so anxious to see Dr. Sutherland. When he came, he told us that the mass of scar tissue was much bigger than he initially thought and that it had attached itself to the bladder. So, he had to take time to slowly and carefully slice out from the outer wall of the bladder to remove the cyst. Then, of course, he had to tie the urinary tube, which had to be cut to get the cyst out, then reconnect that; all the other tubes that were severed also had to be reconnected.

He also advised us that some of the tubes that had to be severed included the one that carries sperm out, meaning that Anzic wouldn't be able to have children. Dr. Sutherland said that Anzic would still be able to enjoy intimacy, but not to have children.

All in all, the surgery was a success, and the doctor told us that Anzic shouldn't have any further infections from that source. I felt so sorry for Anzic in his losing some of the functions of his lower organs, but I was satisfied to hear that the long-standing issue of infection in the urinary tract would now stop. This would mean no more swelling in his lower extremities, and this was a great relief to both my wife and me.

The huge relief for us was that Anzic would be able to live a more normal life, as normal as one can be considering his condition. This gave us hope that Anzic could continue in school upon his return to Palau.

We thanked Dr. Sutherland, and he told us to wait for the nurse who would come and give us further instructions. So, he left, and shortly after that, the nurse came and gave us Anzic's room number and told us that Anzic would be wheeled there shortly. We could go in and wait for him to arrive.

When Anzic was brought into the room where we waited, he was half asleep. He opened his eyes and saw us but paid little attention. I assumed the anesthesia still had its effect on him. He looked tired, heavy-eyed, and in need of sleep. He slept the rest of the day, though my daughters all came to wish him well. We were so grateful for the support, encouragement, prayer, and food that others also provided to get us through this time. This really was the nature of God's family at work. We felt so blessed with Anzic at that time.

The next day, Anzic still seemed very tired and had such sleepy eyes. So, we spent a couple of days just watching Anzic as he slept and slept. On December 24, I attended a gathering at the *Blai er a Omekungil* with Ja-el (O.B.) and Janel (Dilbi). I reported on Anzic's condition and thanked everybody for their prayer and support.

There at Kapi'olani Medical Center, we spent Christmas

together as a family. We cherished this time and felt God's presence so strongly as we surrounded our son. We felt God was most certainly there to comfort us, to share our pain as well as our joys, and to heal Anzic. I had no doubt that Anzic would recover from this surgery, as well as the upcoming hip surgery, because I knew God would be with him. I felt that Jesus's message in John 14:27 was so real at this time: "Peace I leave with you. My peace I give to you. I do not give to you as the world gives; your heart must not be troubled or fearful."

On Christmas Day we had a surprise visitor. Santa Claus came and visited us at the hospital. He brought Anzic big gifts of toy cars, toy airplanes, and teddy bears. Anzic was ecstatic and sang Christmas songs for Santa Claus and his helpers. They all joined in, and we sang together Anzic's favorite Christmas song, "Silent Night." Afterward, he wanted to shake hands with everyone, even being bandaged and with tubes coming out of his arms. Although he was in recovery, what joy and excitement he had with everyone! He made sure he shook hands with everyone—with Santa and his helpers, and even with us who had been with him from the beginning. I was so touched and humbled by all this. Seeing him with such joy in his heart made me realize how God can bring joy to even the lowly ones.

In Psalm 138, David says, "Though the LORD is exalted, he looks kindly on the lowly" (138:6). And Psalm 102:17 says that the Lord "will respond to the prayer of the destitute; he will not despise their plea." God truly cares for all people, and especially for those who really need His help.

On December 27, Anzic was released from Kapi'olani, and we returned to the Shriners Hospital Family Center. Everyone there greeted us enthusiastically, and Anzic was so happy to be back. He wheeled his wheelchair around the room and greeted everyone. They gave Anzic a bag of gifts from Shriners Hospital, Hawaiian Airline, and other donors. The bag was huge and had many toys, including cars and robots. Anzic was so happy he didn't know what to do with it all. So, we took out only some of the toys for him to play with, and we put the others away for our family Christmas party on December 30, when we brought all of our gifts for one another to my daughters' apartment, where we prepared food and had wonderful fellowship. We had many gifts, but most of them were for Anzic.

We greatly enjoyed our Christmas party as a family, being together in that small apartment. We were sort of cramped, but what a joyful time it was.

God had worked out everything for us to be together as a family in beautiful Hawaii. He had used the circumstances to provide what we thought would be impossible. We were together as a family, unlike the previous two Christmases (Balie was in Hawaii to attend school in 2013, and both she and O.B. were there for school in 2014). We were all together, and it was a wonderful time. And had it not been for Anzic, this might not have been possible.

I also knew that there were many more things God was preparing for us through Anzic, and in due time they would be revealed.

Too many operations and too many health problems. But when you are at the bottom, the only place to move is up. With God, it can be done. "I look to the hills - where does my help come from? My help comes from the Lord, the Maker of heaven and earth" (Psalm 121:1).

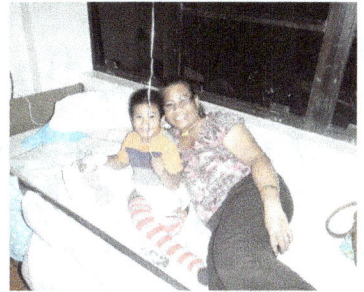

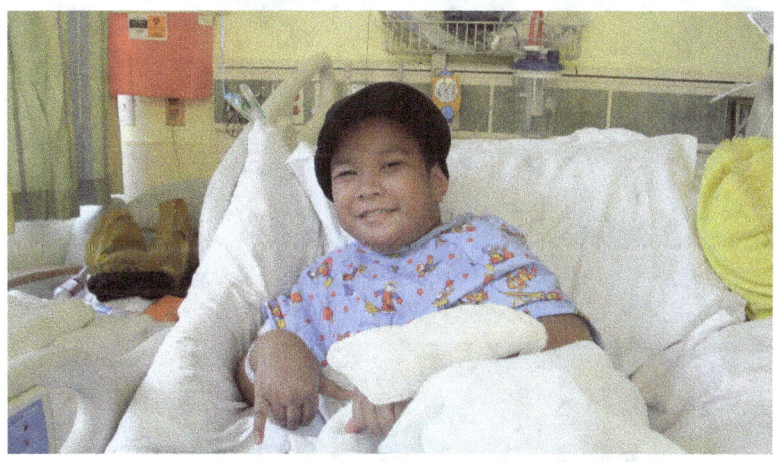

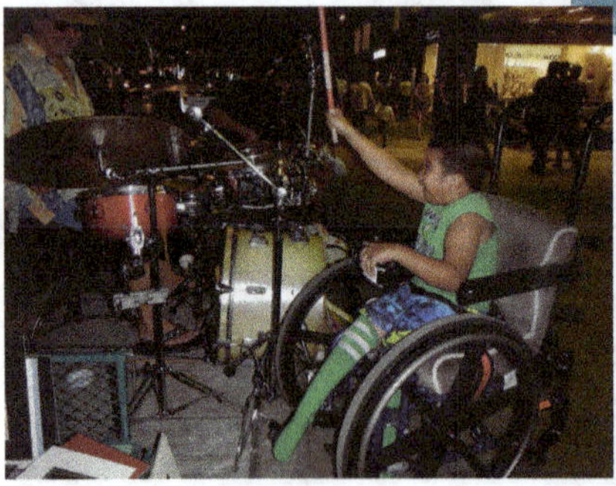

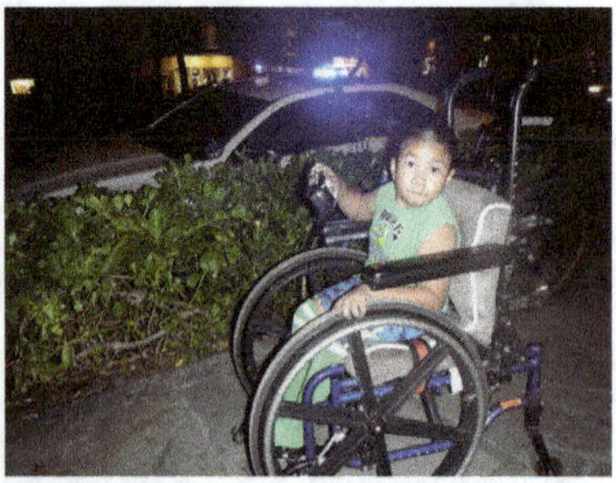

In Hawaii, Anzic had friends at Shriners Hospital. But also, many visitors came to see them, he also was able to ride his wheelchair down to Waikiki and meet with the night performers. He especially enjoyed the Bus ride back to the hospital.

10

The Second Miracle

Anzic's main surgery still lay ahead of us, and it had already been a long journey. We were anxious to have his hip fixed in order to relieve his constant pain. We also hoped that this would enable him to put some weight on his left leg, which would aid him when he crawled.

He'd had surgery in 2013, and the right leg had healed well. But the hardware they'd put in to secure the bones on the left leg had to be removed after it loosened. At the time, the doctors felt that the healing would continue without further intervention, meaning without the brace.

This was not to be the case. Later in 2013, while my wife and I were at a church event, Anzic fell off a couch, and Regina, our Filipina helper, found him on the living room floor. We headed to the hospital once again, where x-rays showed that Anzic had two fractures in his left thigh bone. A visiting specialist said that because of Anzic's eggshell-like bones, Anzic needed to be treated by the better-trained doctors from Hawaii, and he wrote a referral for this for Anzic.

The Shiners doctors were supposed to arrive in Palau shortly, but that particular trip was canceled. It was October 2014, eight months later, when they finally arrived. After examining Anzic, they decided not to take him into their program, since they believed the bones would heal on their own. We accepted their diagnosis.

But Anzic wasn't healing, and it became apparent that he wasn't using his left leg much. Instead, he was heavily favoring the right leg.

The Shriners doctors returned in July of 2015, and the

young doctor who examined Anzic again told us that they weren't taking him into the program. At that point, I became upset and wanted to know why. I told them that Anzic was in constant pain and I wanted to know if they were going to allow that to continue.

From the x-rays, I could see that the part of the bone that had been broken earlier to have the ball of the thighbone inserted in the hip socket was clearly separated from the longer femur bone. To me, it appeared that it was pushing against the flesh toward his stomach. I was also concerned that it might pierce something or interfere with his other organs. So, I told the doctor looking at Anzic that I wanted him to reassess Anzic's case, and to consider taking him back and fixing him, because I could see that he was always in pain. So, the doctor made arrangements for Anzic to see the head doctor of the team in the afternoon.

When we returned in the afternoon, the other doctor, along with the head of the delegation, came and looked at Anzic and at his x-rays. He immediately noticed that there were two fractures in the same bone—one right above the knee, and the one that they'd broken to insert the ball joint into the socket. These didn't look so well. After a short discussion with the team, he told us that Anzic had to be taken to Hawaii and have his legs fixed again. We agreed and asked that it be done soon because he was always in pain.

On October 7, 2015, we finally left Palau and headed toward Hawaii. This would be the third time Anzic would be traveling to Hawaii for surgery on his legs.

After the other treatments, Anzic finally had clearance from Dr. Sutherland to proceed with the hip surgery for which he originally came. This is what we had traveled to Hawaii for in October of 2015. However, it was now January of 2016.

But before the hip surgery could happen, my wife had to meet with Dr. Moroz, Anzic's operating physician, and discuss the surgery for Anzic. I wasn't able to be there for this meeting. However, whenever we could, my wife and I were talking on Skype and discussing the surgery, to give me peace of mind about the treatment. I was very concerned, because she told me that the doctors might not be able to save the short femur bone. She said the doctor was concerned that the shorter bone that was left after the dislocation might not have grown stronger and might not have grown at the same rate as the longer femur bone. If that were the case, then the doctors would have no choice but to remove the shorter bone. That would mean Anzic wouldn't be able to use his left leg at all because the bones wouldn't be connected. She asked if I could return to Hawaii and talk to Doctor Moroz.

So again, I flew to Hawaii. When we met Dr. Moroz, he explained the risks and possibilities and his concerns. I immediately turned to God in prayer. It was suddenly clear to both my wife and me: we gave our permission without reservation, and we told him we would proceed following his lead and his knowledge. I also told him that I couldn't stay in Hawaii, but my wife would be there. My wife and I agreed that whatever Dr. Moroz decided, we would take that as the best for our son at this stage. He gave us an expression reflecting his appreciation for this vote of confidence and support we were giving him. This also gave us some comfort and confidence that Dr. Moroz would be led by the Lord and would do what was best for Anzic.

During the surgery, which was done on February 10, 2016, the bone that had moved—which caused the postponement of the original surgery date on November 10—surprisingly was found to be back in its original position! This enabled Dr. Moroz to connect the two bones and brace it with hardware.

My wife called me and reported on the surgery and told me they were able to save the bone. There had been so many miracles one after another during Anzic's treatment that we immediately knew this was yet another miracle from God.

The fact that the shorter femur bone was back in its original position, and the saving of it, meant that it was strong enough to take the brace.

We simply praised God that He demonstrated His love and care for this young boy by making sure everything was done right for him. All had been taken out of our hands, and we had been powerless to decide, perform, or change anything. God had put everything in motion for Anzic, and the whole family was in it for the ride only. Everything God did was for Anzic's good and ours as well.

God told his people in Exodus 15:26, "If you will give earnest heed to the voice of the Lord your God, and do what is right in His sight, and give ear to His commandments, and keep all His statutes, I will put none of the diseases on you which I have put on the Egyptians; for I, the Lord, am your Healer." I felt that we had hit rock bottom, that we had no choice. And God came through. But I'm also reminded by this verse that when my wife and I and even my older daughters Balie and O.B., hit rock bottom for Anzic, God came through with his good plans for him. We also noted that we sought God and examined our lives to ensure we followed His commands.

In Psalm 20:6, David says, "Now I am sure that the Lord will deliver his chosen king; he will intervene for him from his holy heavenly temple and display his mighty ability to deliver." What a wonderful God! He does have the ability to deliver. No wonder Jesus said, "Come unto me, all you who labor and are heavy laden, and I will give you rest." He most certainly is able.

It had taken us time to see that the Lord was indeed in control, and this made me realize how small my faith was. As many times as God had shown us His great and awesome power, still I failed to see His work, and I continued to question things, trying to interject my ideas or intervene in His work. No wonder Jesus says, "If you have faith the size of a mustard seed, if you say to this mountain, 'Go there,' it will be so. Nothing will be impossible to you" (Matthew 17:20-21).

Many stories in the Bible reminded me of how great men of faith were able to recognize God's work and to believe almost instantly. Such a man was King David, who continued to amaze me. No wonder he was "a man after God's own heart." Imagine a man having been anointed as the next king of Israel, and yet he had to run for his life from the man he was to replace. During that time, he had several opportunities to take Saul's life and to save himself, his men, and even Israel from further ruin because of Saul's removal from God's grace (1 Samuel 23 and 26). It seemed like this would have been better for everyone. However, each time King Saul became vulnerable, David saved him by ordering his men not to touch him. The interaction between David, Saul, and God reflected one person who had lost God's grace (and whom God no longer answered or supported), and another who strongly trusted God no matter in whatever circumstances.

When David was a fugitive from Saul, he would have loved to live in a house and enjoy the peace that every man pursues. But he also knew that God has plans, and those plans are good no matter how difficult your life becomes. I believe this was the inspiration that enabled David to write, "Trust in the Lord and do good, dwell in the land and enjoy safe pasture, delight yourself in the Lord, and He will give you the desires of your heart" (Psalm 37:3-4).

I realized that Anzic's condition and his treatment were all out of my hands. I simply had to trust God in all that. I also had to acknowledge that God sent Anzic's condition, and I needed to thank Him and praise Him for it, no matter how painful it was to know that he would never be able to enjoy life as a normal child would. I needed to believe God and His Word. If we trusted in the Lord and delighted in Him, He would give us the desires of our hearts—even when they didn't appear to match my expectations.

I realized how lacking I was in my trust in the Lord. I still relied on my own abilities and what I could see and what I could reach. I realized that I constantly worried, and when I could change the situation, I would. I really needed to deal with the issue of faith in my life.

Then I realized I could learn a lot from Anzic. When I looked at my son, I saw that he simply accepted what was coming. He put his full trust in whatever we said or did. If we told him we would go for a walk later, he would look forward to when you came and said, "Let's go." He hardly ever complained, questioned, or made a fuss. But your word must be kept; your commitments must be carried out. Anzic held us to our word and let us know his disappointment when we didn't follow through on what we had promised.

When you realize that someone really depends on you and that you'll be a blessing to them if you're true to your word—you work extra hard to make sure you fulfill your commitments.

I also realized I could even learn from Anzic's negative reactions. He does get irritated or angry after having waited patiently, often for more than an hour, for something, and the plans are then changed. Other things that irritated him were when his sister, Dilbi, wouldn't share the Samsung tablet, or when those who promised him something don't show any sign of carrying through on their commitment. In fact, his reactions to this would be quite strong.

At these times, I could see myself in Anzic's shoes when he'd lost patience and became demanding. Often, I wouldn't wait upon the Lord to answer. I often asked for something from God and hoped to get an instant positive answer from Him. When I didn't get it, I would question whether God was real, or was even able to grant such a request. In my church work at Koror Evangelical Church, and especially with the church youth, I often see many people who have convinced themselves that God cannot do certain things. They speak of experiences when they asked God for something, and they didn't get it. Often, I find out that what they asked for was something that demanded an immediate response from God.

God is faithful and wants us to lean on Him, to delight in Him, and to trust Him. I feel that if we do so, He will give us what we desire. Anzic lives by relying on others; he trusts that we will give him what he wants, and he waits patiently for it. We, too, should live patiently trusting God, doing good, and delighting ourselves in Him, and He will grant us what we want in His time and in His way.

After the two successful operations in Hawaii, one for the cyst and the other for the left hip, Anzic started recovery on his way to enjoying life as it was meant to be.

Anzic at the Dole Plantation waiting for the train ride, playing with the birds at the Sea Life Park, and the Shriners family that has been loving and best of friends.

Family Christmas and with the Church Youth Shalom at the Rock Island. 2017.

11

God's Purpose and Will

During one of Anzic's confinements at the Belau National Hospital for an infection, a group of young Christians came for a very welcome visit. They sang songs, and one of the young men started to tell us how he was going to pray for Anzic, and that if we believed, Anzic would rise and walk.

Not wanting to argue with him, I kept quiet and simply listened to him. Then he told me that Anzic's condition was because of sin, and we must denounce that sin.

I started some soul-searching. What kind of sin had brought this to Anzic? I could see that my wife was starting to get agitated by that young man, who then told me that I had to believe, and if I didn't believe, then the prayer he would offer for Anzic's healing wouldn't work. He told me that he himself believed, and his small group all believed, and this was why they came to the hospital to pray. But now it was up to us. If we believed, then Anzic would be healed, because the Bible said so. He cited the faith as illustrated in Matthew 17:20, where Jesus said, "Because you have so little faith. I tell you the truth, if you have faith as small as a mustard seed, you can say to this mountain, 'Move from here to there,' and it will move. Nothing will be impossible to you."

By this time, I started to feel like the young man was shifting the burden to me. He would pray a prayer of faith, and if it didn't work and Anzic wasn't able to walk, I would be blamed for lacking the faith to heal my son.

Still not wanting to get into a theological confrontation, I quietly told the young man that God still performs miracles, but He does so for His own purpose and glory. I cited the story in John 9, where Jesus and his disciples came across a blind man who has been blind since birth. His disciples asked him, "Rabbi, who sinned, this man or his parents, that he is born blind?" And Jesus said, "Neither this man nor his parents sinned. But this happened so that the work of God may be displayed in this life. As long as it is day, we must do the work of him who sent me. Night is coming, when no one can work" (John 9:1-4).

Whether the young man really meant with all his heart that he was going to heal Anzic despite the medical advice that we had received from doctors, I wasn't so sure. Yet I wanted to examine my faith to see if I could actually believe God would heal Anzic so he could be normal like any other young boy. I also searched my life and begged forgiveness for everything I'd ever done against anyone, or against God, or even against my children.

One thing for sure was that this young man made me think a lot about Anzic, and about what he meant to all of us, and what his role was in our relationship with God. Somewhere in the back of mind, I knew that God has a purpose for Anzic. Rick Warren, in his book *The Purpose Driven Life*, says in chapter 2 that we are not accidents. He goes on to say that "long before we are conceived by our parents, we are conceived in the mind of God." "It is not fate, nor chance, nor luck, nor coincidence..." that we are born into this world.[1] Rev. Warren cites Psalm 139:15-16, which says, "My frame was not hidden from you when I was made in the secret place. When I was woven together in the depths of the earth. Your eyes saw my unformed body and all the days ordained for me were written in your book" (NIV). Deep down inside I know that God knew all along about Anzic. And I knew that for me to not accept Anzic for who he is, would derail me from what God intended for me through his disability. And I know that what he intended

---

1   *The Purpose Driven Life, Rick Warren, Zondervan, 2002, page 22-23)*

for me is good for me as well as for Anzic. Going back to verse 14 of the same chapter of the book of Psalms, it says, "I praise you because I am fearfully and wonderfully made, your works are wonderful. I know that full well" (NIV). I knew that the God of the universe was going to awaken my faith and strengthen my relationship with Him through Anzic's disability. I knew that God's intentions are all good and my son and I would benefit from His grace, love, and blessings, even through Anzic's disability.

I looked at the young man and said, "God would heal Anzic or not according to *His* will and for *His* glory and purpose, and not according to what you or I desire or possess in terms of faith." The young man insisted that it all depended on me. If I had faith, Anzic would get up and walk after he prayed, but if I didn't have enough faith, then he would remain in his current state. So, I asked him if Paul didn't have enough faith to heal his ailments—his "thorn in the flesh." The young man's response was short and straight: "I am not concerned about Paul, but about your son. And the Bible says if we have faith, whatever we ask of the Father in the name of Jesus, He will give us." I gave up and simply asked him to just pray.

This one little event kept coming back to me. What was Anzic's role in all of our lives? Was he to remind us of our weaknesses before God? Were we also this handicap in front of Him? And I thought, "The answer is yes." We were powerless without Jesus, and only He could restore us back to God and sustain us in our faith.

I went back and studied Paul's text in 2 Corinthians 12:7-10: "To keep me from becoming conceited because of these surpassingly great revelations, there was given to me a thorn in the flesh, a messenger of Satan, to torment me. Three times I pleaded with the Lord to take it away from me. But he said to me, *'My grace is sufficient for you, for my power is made perfect in weakness.'* Therefore, I will boast all the more gladly about my weaknesses so that Christ's power may rest on me. That is why, for Christ's sake, I delight in weaknesses, in insults, in hardships, in persecutions, in difficulties. For when I am weak, then I am strong."

What a profound statement by Paul, but most certainly contrary to our modern-day culture. People don't want to show their weaknesses. People don't want any weaknesses in their lives. They want to feel strong, and they preach strong. Such terms as *strong economy, strong will,* and *only the strong survive* are part of our everyday talk. We most certainly don't want to appear weak or let anyone know we have any weaknesses. But Paul says that by being weak, we rely on God's strength to sustain us, and we become strong. For that reason, Paul was happy to have weaknesses and difficulties, because in all that, God's strength was there to help him.

Something always told me that Anzic was not a mistake and that God didn't make a mistake by bringing him into this world and into our family. As a son, we love him, but to understand his purpose humbles us and makes us appreciate him even more. His condition reminds me that we aren't to be conceited. We have to constantly rely on God in all our limitations and challenges. Anzic is a constant reminder that our spiritual development and growth is mirrored in his life. The state of our spiritual health is just like Anzic's physical condition. No matter how strong and developed we are spiritually, we still need God. The more we show weakness, the more God will show His strength.

Moses must have felt like a huge failure—a handicap, so to speak. Every time he confronted Pharaoh, he and the Israelites suffered more—from one challenge to another—and Pharaoh would throw the blame on Moses. As a result, Moses saw the Israelites, his own people, turning against him. Every time he served God faithfully by delivering His message and performing a miracle, the Egyptians and his own people turned against him. But the more he confronted Pharaoh, the more he grew in faith. He understood God was doing the battle for him, and God would not let him down. He didn't fear Pharaoh anymore; he knew that God would deliver, just as He had promised. Moses became more courageous and bolder in his confrontations. He also became more authoritative with the Israelites as he realized that he and his work and actions were in line with God's will. The more Moses realized that he could do nothing, the more he understood that God will perform through him.

With Anzic, I realize that the more I try to do, the more I move away from God's purpose. But the more I understand my limitations and turn to God, the more God will show His strength through my weakness.

When I look at Anzic and observe him, he understands and knows very well that he cannot do much without the help of others. He embraces any help that comes his way. It's through this help that he can do and accomplish the things he wants. But Anzic understands his limitations and doesn't seek things that are beyond his reach. When we ask him to do more than he can do, he will look at us and shake his head, knowing he cannot do it.

We, too, need to know that spiritually and even physically we cannot do much without relying on God. Moses never would have been able to get the people out of Egypt if not for God's intervention. He never would have been able to successfully lead the people of Israel for forty years in the wilderness without God's help.

On this earth, we are like wanderers in the wilderness. We own nothing, and we will leave with nothing. What matters is how we utilize the help that comes our way. Jesus said, "I am the true vine and you are the branches. If a man remains in me and I in him, he will bear much fruit. Apart from me you can do nothing" (John 15:5). A part of me wants Anzic to be healed and to be whole like every normal kid. After all, he's our only son! We want him to play sports. We want him to be able to go fishing. We want him to be his mom's helper in the garden. I want him to be my fishing partner.

But the other part of me wants him just as he is—to constantly remind me of how much I need God each day of my life, just like Anzic needs someone each day of his life.

This trip to Hawaii, in which God enabled me to escort my wife and Anzic, opened my eyes as to Anzic's purpose and to our purpose for living for God. Before this, I'd been too busy with work and work-related travels that I didn't appreciate the value of family. But on this trip, the blessings were so obvious and just stood out, and it was hard not to notice.

I began to consider and recount these blessings. The first one was that God enabled my wife's brother, who worked for the airlines, to enroll me as his enrolled friend at the beginning of 2015. This enabled me to travel to Hawaii in February to see our daughters, Balie and O.B., and to familiarize myself with the landscape of Honolulu and its dynamic culture. In April, God blessed me with a trip to the Asia Pacific Center for Security Studies right in Waikiki. Participating in this program for six weeks, I became familiar with the roads, the stores, and so forth.

Then, because I was an enrolled friend of my wife's brother (my brother-in-law), I was able to travel with her and Anzic when he was finally accepted by Shriners Hospital for treatment of his legs. This was a blessing both for my wife and me and also for Anzic, because during transit in Guam, we missed our flight to Honolulu and had to spend the night in Guam. Since I know my way around Guam as I have been there numerous times before and am able to drive there, I was able to get a rental car and shop for Anzic, because our checked-in luggage had all been flown to Hawaii. If I hadn't been there, it would have been a nightmare for my wife, since she doesn't drive in Guam and is not familiar with the roads and stores in Guam. Both she and Anzic would have starved in their hotel room.

Before that, and before the Shriners doctors accepted Anzic for treatment there, Anzic had his series of serious infections of the scrotum area. He'd spent a number of weeks in the hospital while taking antibiotics to kill the bacteria in his body. These infections became so numerous that he missed the entire school year of 2015-2016. Since the doctors in Palau weren't able to detect the cause of the infections, they recommended that we ask the doctors at Shriners Hospital to look into it and prescribe the right treatment. However, Shriners Hospital specializes in orthopedic care for children who have problems with their bones, and they don't deal with or focus on infections or urology problems.

Shriners Hospital was prepared to treat only his bone problem—his dislocated hip—and not the infection issue. But twice, when they got him ready for surgery for the dislocated hip, something came up and the surgery was postponed. After the second postponement, Anzic had a severe case of infection that had to be dealt with by a specialist. He was taken to Kapi'olani Medical Center, and there he had the surgery, and the infection was stopped. We believe that the trip to Kapi'olani, and the surgery to remove a cyst in his bladder, were all God's plan and blessing to Anzic and to us. Furthermore, God enabled Med-QUEST, a state program to help pay for emergency medical bills for Hawaii residents, to pay for the entire cost.

As we prepared to return home, I now could clearly see how God continually blesses us in abundance. Most often we fail to recognize it or appreciate it. But He does. Yes, He performs miracles even today, and especially for children with disabilities.

Anzic brings out the sympathy of most people who observe him—his classmates, his teachers, our relatives, fellow church members, and many others. They see his outward appearance and realize that he's constrained. But his spirit is not constrained! He's free like a bird and so full of life and joy. He can sit on the floor all day and watch TV and play with his cars without a single complaint. He's able to lie down and go to sleep and to wake up and do the same all over again. Most people are unable to do that.

Anzic's wheelchair is a sign of his confinement. But Anzic's reach is far beyond the wheelchair. His personality, his spirit, and his character take him far beyond what many normal children are able to reach. His condition enables him to approach anyone, open conversations with anyone, get anyone to help him, and get anyone to like him with his dear smile. He makes friends everywhere he goes. In school, he's so well liked that sometimes he asks the kids to give him space, because they're always around him.

The world has come up with many different names for children like Anzic—disabled, handicapped, special needs. To us, Anzic is simply a special child, not because of his needs, but because of what he uncovers in our lives. He demonstrates a life that's in constant reliance on our Creator, the greatest designer of life. And I believe that we're truly blessed because of who Anzic is. God brought him to our lives to demonstrate His blessings to us and to open our eyes to His miracles that He performs every day for us.

We hope that you, too, have been blessed by sharing in Anzic's life through this book. If you have a child with a disability, that child has a far greater purpose in God's grand plan for you and for that child. Look to God for help, and He will provide divine support like you've never seen before. He is a God of love and a God of miracles. Jesus Christ is the living proof of that.

Please read John 3:16, where it says, "For God so loved the world that He gave his one and only Son, that whoever believes in Him will not perish but will have eternal life." Also read John 1:12, where it says, "But as many as received Him, those who believed in His name, to them He gave the power to be called the children of God."

Post-Surgery Therapy photos

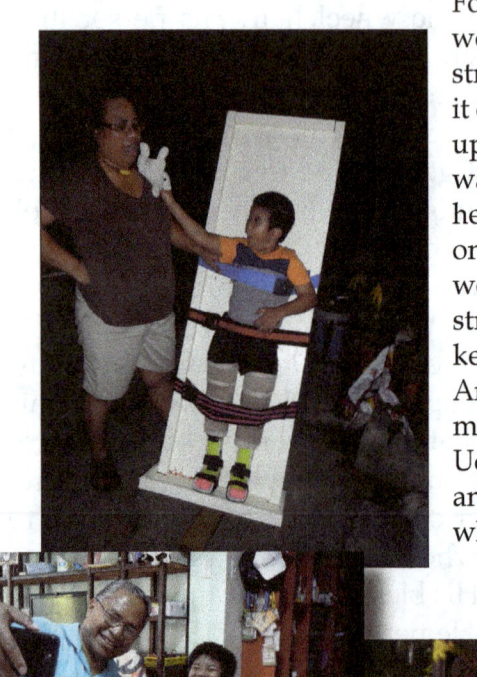

For Anzic's therapy, we made a make shift stretcher with hinges so it can be brought to an upright position. This was necessary because he needed to put weight on his legs to get them to work. This would help strengthen his legs and keep the growth going. Anzic exercises with mom, a rare visit Deacon Uchel Naito of Hawaii and riding his outdoor wheelchair by the beach.

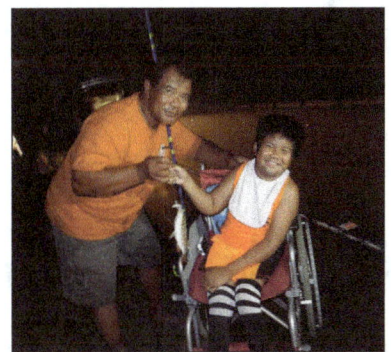

Anzic on his mobile wheelchair catching a fish on Independence Day with dad. Anzic enjoys his new stand-up wheelchair.

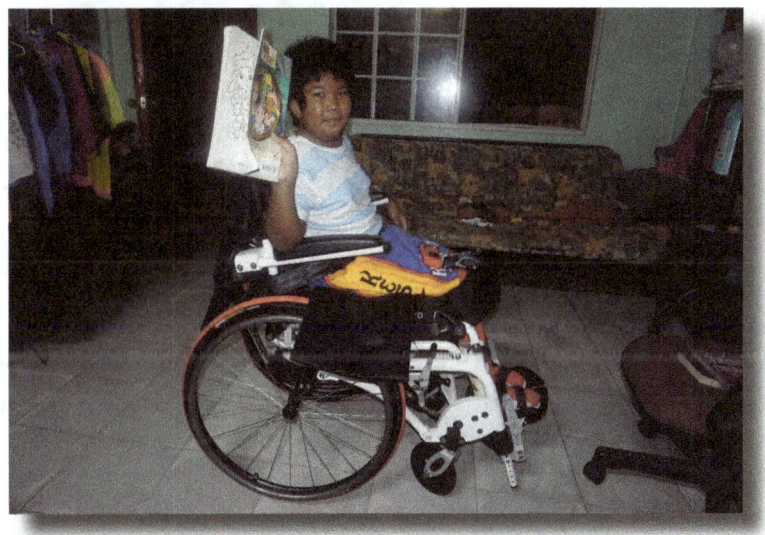

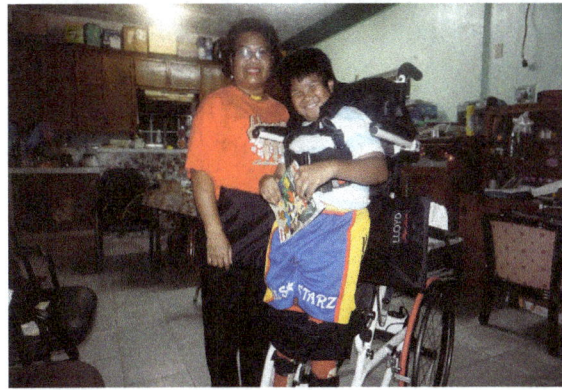

Anzic exercising with mom on his standup Pegasus II wheelchair purchased with funds from Australia Direct Aid Program (DAP).

12

About This Book's Title

I've titled this book *The Miracle of the Hermit Crab*, which deserves a little explaining. The hermit crab is a small and rather odd-looking creature living along the seashore. This crab is about a quarter of an inch in length. Except for its claws and legs, its body is soft and vulnerable to predators. To find protection, it finds an empty shell and inserts its body, making the shell its home. The shell becomes a hard armor that shields the crab from predators while allowing it to still use its claws for defense.

When my daughters Balie and O.B. (Jael) attended Bethania High School in the Ngaraard State of Babeldaob, we often went to visit them. Bethania is a girls' boarding school beautifully situated beside a long stretch of sandy beach, with many hermit crabs residing on the shoreline. Whenever we went to visit, we would collect hermit crabs for Anzic, as he enjoyed playing with them.

Sometimes I would feel sorry for the crabs, because whenever Anzic lets them go, they try to escape his reach by crawling away as fast as they can. However, since they're small, it takes them some time to escape Anzic's reach. He often watches them with glee, and when he realizes they're almost out of reach, he stretches out his arms to catch and bring them back.

Watching all this more closely, I realized that the hermit crabs are pretty much like Anzic. They're tiny, vulnerable, and weak. They don't move very fast and can't really escape any predator. For protection and safety, they have to rely on outside strength, like the borrowed shell on their back. The shell-home serves as a shield and protector.

I also observed how a hermit crab hangs around the shore, waiting for anything that washes up, so it can grab a meal. It never seems to run out of food, as many things wash up on the shore. It's a very dependent creature, yet all its needs are provided. Likewise, I could see that Anzic's disability and physical challenges—especially his disorder which required treatment—were a constant demonstration of his vulnerability and weakness. In Anzic's state of being so dependent, God came through for him and provided all the support he needed, and more.

I also realized that I am vulnerable and weak, just like Anzic. We all are. We're totally helpless in many ways in life, and if we think about it carefully, we realize that many challenges are beyond our strength and abilities to resolve.

Anzic's miracle was not only the treatments he received. It is his whole life. His entire life enables those who look through a Christian lens to see God's handiwork of miracles.

God performs miracles in our lives as well. Those miracles are not only to heal us or keep us from sickness and other afflictions; they're also present to ensure that we fulfill God's purpose in our lives. In Zechariah 4:6 we read, "Not by might, nor by power, but by my Spirit, says the Lord." It's not by our own strength and might that we live godly lives, but through the power of God's spirit. Anzic lives and survives by God's Spirit enabling him to be who he is today.

The life of hermit crabs is that of miracles. They depend on a shell for protection and leftovers for meals. They may not be fast, nor are they strong, nor are they smart (or maybe they are), but they live to fulfill their purpose within their own world.

Two years later

The beginning of 2018 marked two years after Anzic's major cyst surgery and hip surgery. These were his fourth and fifth surgeries. We have been keeping our eyes on him for any major change, side effects, or new development. In the meantime, he is back at Koror Elementary School in the Special Education Program. We truly appreciate his teachers, as they have shown great love for him and have been extremely patient in teaching and caring for him. He has a few classmates with whom he enjoys playing and attending classes. He participates in activities and field trips with +these classmates. He seems oblivious to the fact that just two years ago, his life had been a major roller coaster ride of illnesses, infections, and pain. He seems to focus on studying and school activities.

In July 2017, a team of doctors and support staff from the Shriners hospital came to Palau. His operating doctor was with the group, and so we were very excited to see him and hear of his assessment after the year of recovery. When we prepared Anzic to go to the hospital, he was very excited to go. When we got to the hospital, he was excited to see all the people there and especially those in wheelchairs who were also there to see the Shriners doctors. Anzic had his screening and enjoyed rolling his wheelchair around while we waited to see the doctor.

After the initial screening, we were called in and told that Anzic had to have his X-ray taken. We expected this, as it is always done when the doctors come for a visit. We were a bit anxious about the X-ray because he often didn't like it. But this time, he had no trouble with it. He cooperated fully, and we laid him down on the X-ray table. I laid there next to him with my lead armor, and they took the X-rays of his legs and hips from several different angles. He seemed unbothered and enjoyed talking to the technicians and staff. This day, he seemed energized, perhaps because he has been cooped up in the house for too long and felt excited to be among many people. Perhaps the hospital environment was a change of pace from our neighborhood—where we often take him to stroll around—or the church parking lot and schoolyard. In those places, there are few people. But

I do remember that he looks for people, and whenever he sees some, he has to stop by and talk to them or at least say hi. So, he liked the hospital setting, with many people around, including some in wheelchairs.

Since returning from Hawaii in 2016, we have stopped bringing Anzic to church and to big gatherings. He had an increasing dislike of sounds like coughs, clearing throats, and small clicking sounds of cell phones, which led to a greater level of annoyance and anger. He would get to the point where he would slowly wheel his chair next to someone who coughed and suddenly spring into action and pinch and scream at the person. While his attacks didn't induce a lot of pain, it does take the person by surprise. When they laughed, I believe mostly at themselves for being surprised, Anzic would really get mad. So, to avoid him trying to hurt someone, we would keep him home. In church, many people clear their throats or cough before they sing, and this really makes him angry. He would argue with us to take him outside or even take him home. He would get so irritated that he would remember the people who made the noises. If we brought him to church the following Sunday, and he sees someone he remembers coughed or made those annoying noises, he would move quietly next to them and then attack them. This surprises people, and when they look at him, somehow, they think it is funny, and they laugh, which makes him even angrier.

Many times, we would get to church only to be asked to go back home. And this really creates a problem for me because often I have preaching duties or other responsibilities related to the program. So, going back home and returning often causes me to be late. So, to please him and everyone else, we decided just to keep him home. We do bring him to church on Christmas, Easter, and other programs where the children at church have presentations. At home, he enjoys watching TBN and the singing of church songs on the channel.

Back to the hospital waiting room, the patients were just kids with physical challenges and not illnesses that cause them to cough. So, he also enjoyed wheeling himself around and interacting with everyone. It was also good because he chose to wheel himself around; often, he would simply sit and asks someone to push him around. The doctors finally came and called for Anzic. He seemed excited to go in and screamed with glee. Once in, he seemed to recognize his doctor, which made him stop and give that long look as if he were trying to remember where he had seen the doctor. We wheeled him into the treatment room and removed him from the wheelchair and laid him on the table. His doctor came and examined his legs, and once he touched his legs, I think he remembered. He immediately said "no, no, no" and told me that he wanted me to put him back in his wheelchair.

We eventually realized that after one year, he still remembers his doctor and the pain that he went through. While there was very little pain in his operations because he was sedated, the encounter still triggered his response of wanting to leave or get away from that hospital. Once we put him back in his wheelchair, he immediately wanted to get back to the lobby and waiting area where there were many children.

The doctor reported to us that Anzic's bone was healing well, but he chose to leave on the metal bone brace, which held the fractured left hip bone in place to facilitate healing, for another year. The doctor wanted it to remain to make sure the healing is complete. He reported that Anzic seemed to be doing well and would eventually be able to put some weight on both legs. But he still wouldn't be able to walk.

In 2018, the doctors came in the same month of July. When we told Anzic that we were going to go and see his doctor, he really became excited. He told his babysitter that I was taking him on the airplane to see his doctor. That surprised me that would think that. I wondered if he remembered going to Hawaii for treatment and that was the reason for all the excitement. Regardless, when I told him that we were not going on the airplane, but simply on a car to the local hospital, he didn't show any sign of disappointment. He was still excited about going out and perhaps seeing other people. When we drove up to the hospital, he could not contain his excitement. He was singing and laughing and really showed excitement. Once inside the lobby where all the children were, he was very happy, just like the previous year where he seemed to really enjoy the company of other children with ailments like him.

We allowed him to roam around and greet the other children and their parents. He would shake hands with everyone and appeared to try and tell them a story. When he was called in for screening, he volunteered his hand and arm for a checkup and even had fun with the X-ray technicians and staff. When we were finally called by the doctors from the Shriners Hospital, I was concerned that he might have the same reaction as he did the previous year. When we got close to the treatment room, there was the hesitancy again as though he expected something dreadful. He peeked inside and saw the doctor, but this time, the doctor was a lady. He immediately shouted with excitement and proceeded to wheel himself inside. He immediately began to try and tell his story to the doctor. When we took him off the wheelchair and laid him on the examination table, he didn't seem to mind. In fact, it appears that he wanted the doctor to look at him and examine his limbs. We were so relieved.

The doctor looked at him and explained that she had seen the X-rays and feels like Anzic should begin some exercises. We also agreed that we felt he should exercise so this was good news to us. We felt that his legs were starting to gain strength if the doctor felt that exercise will do him some good. Anzic had already started doing that on his own as he would often rise to a kneeling position and then stand on his knees. This puts weight on his hip and on his legs, which is what the doctors wanted. They felt it would give his bones strength if he did it more often. We are now exercising him every day.

We are simply amazed at how God has demonstrated his love and grace to our son Anzic and to those around him, including us. Before the surgery in 2016, the doctors told us that since his last surgery was in 2013, and then after that, the bones were separated and didn't heal properly, they may be different in size. If this is the case, it would be hard to put them together. Also, because it has been almost three years that they have not been functional, it may be difficult to connect them as one may be dead already (no growth). But the surgery in 2016 seems to have resulted in the bones being able to connect and growing normally. During his exercises, we are able to put him on a stand, and he can put weight on those legs and doesn't feel any discomfort. We understand that he still needs to learn how to use them since he's never had to do that before. Of course, we don't expect him to walk, but God is proving that he has plans and will fulfill them despite our lack of faith.

But again, we didn't agree for these surgeries to be performed on Anzic so that he could walk. If God chooses to make him walk that would be great. But we are happy for him as he is, and we are blessed to be taking care of him. We are very proud and happy that for the last two years, since his operation, he has not shown any signs of infection nor pain on his bones. This is a major improvement, and it makes everyone happy for him.

I am reminded of John chapter 9 and the story of the man born blind and the argument of the disciples as to whose sin caused this mishap on the poor man. We all tend to believe that if there is evil, sin, disability, or abnormality, then it must be a curse. A curse can only be caused by sin. If a curse isn't caused by sin, then the God we are taught is just, loving, merciful and full of grace is definitely an unjust God.

About This Book's Title

It would be the only plausible explanation for what causes some to have misfortune and disability while others don't. This view is not shared by only a handful of people but by many. It is the reason for people refusing to believe in God and refusing to search for the real truth about God. They see the world as unfair, using as examples those people who are good people but end up with disabled children; cheaters become wealthy while honest people struggle; deceivers become successful in economics, politics, and businesses while honest and good public servants seem to fail; outlaws and lawbreakers are received as heroes while pastors and church leaders are seen as critics and therefore rejected.

Is God really unfair? Is He sometimes unjust in some cases? Was Anzic one of those unjust situations? If you have a child with a disability, do you see God as unjust? Psalm 117:12 says, "The Lord is righteous in all his ways and loving to all he has made." It also says in Psalm 111:7, "The works of his hand are faithful and just; all his precepts are trustworthy." The Bible makes it clear that God is just, fair, and righteous in all that he does.

Having been with Anzic for the last three years has really opened my eyes to God's love, and grace. It might not have been made apparent if it wasn't for Anzic's disability. For that, I am forever grateful. Every day, I have been able to see God beckoning us to come to him with open and loving arms. Those who find him, find the true meaning of life and are able to see who he really is and how he truly cares for each of us. With this understanding, you will read John 3:16 with a new perspective. Instead of focusing our attention on 'not perish,' but focus on the phrase 'will have eternal life,' you will notice 'the one and only son' and how he achieved that for us. No one who is willing to sacrifice his own son to save the people he loves is willing to serve injustice to the same people. Jesus died on the cross, the cruelest and most shameful death, for us, including Anzic. His victory was achieved not only for the healthy but also for those with disabilities. His love and care resonates every day with one miracle after another.

That is the same for Anzic. His life is a miracle. And we have been blessed tremendously and have grown as Christians by being a part of his life. Don't go through life thinking that all bad things are nothing but a curse to you and your family. Turn to Jesus Christ, because He healed the sick, made the lame walk, made the blind see, made the dumb speak, and made the deaf hear. He even raised the dead, like Lazarus (in John 11). He can do the same for you and your family. He says, "I am the way, the truth, and the life. No man comes to the Father except through Me" (John 14:6). Going to Him, you'll find life and a purpose that will make everything clear for you. It did for Anzic, and it did for me.

God bless you.

About This Book's Title

Palau Disaster Preparedness Parade participated by NGO's and Government agencies

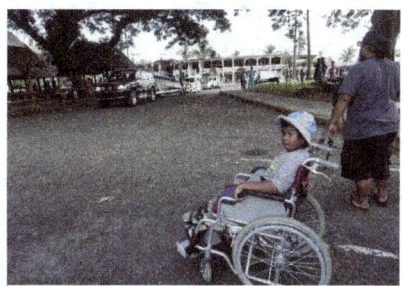
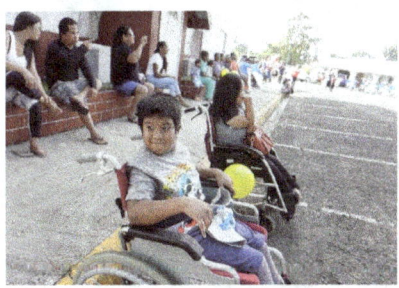
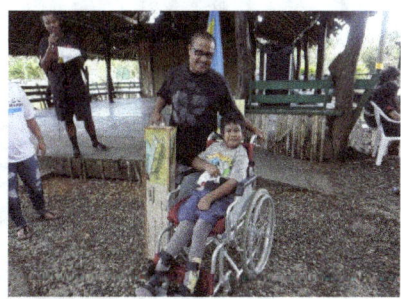

On September 15, 2018, Anzic and his family joined the **Palau Disaster Preparedness** Parade as part of the Omekesang Group (a group for disabled people). During the ceremony's raffle drawing, Anzic won an Army sleeping cot. Anzic was so excited and happy to be a part of this parade, and when he returned home, he would line up his cars and call it his parade. We were all very happy for him and his friends.

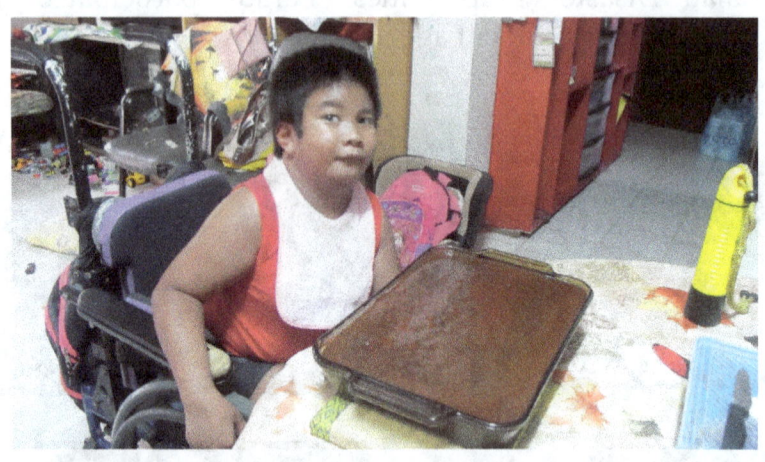

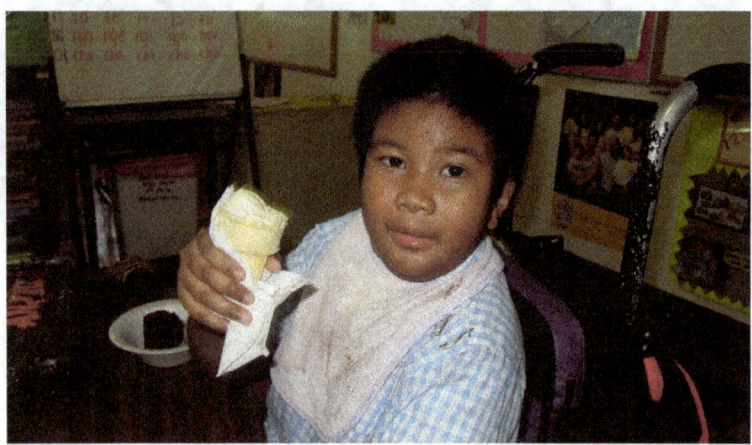

Anzic celebrated his 11th birthday on April 08, 2018 in his classroom at Koror Elementary School, Palau.

THANK YOU FOR READING MY BOOK. I HOPE YOU HAVE BEEN BLESSED.

www.ingramcontent.com/pod-product-compliance
Lightning Source LLC
Chambersburg PA
CBHW052057070526
44584CB00017B/2222